Polished Pages

A Comprehensive Checklist for Cleaning Up Your MS Word Manuscript

Polished Pages

A Comprehensive Checklist for Cleaning Up Your MS Word Manuscript

Wendy Spurlin

www.armlinhouse.com

ArmLin House

ArmLin House Productions
P.O. Box 2522, Littleton, Colorado 80161-2522
www.armlinhouse.com

ISBN: 978-1-958185-36-0

Cover Design by Wendy Spurlin Designs
www.wendyspurlin.art

Printed in the United States of America

First Edition

For everyone who has lost countless hours,
fixing word processor formatting issues!

Contents

Introduction

I F YOU PICKED up this book, it's likely you're working with a manuscript filled with blank spaces and inconsistent punctuation, to say the least.

Whether you're an experienced author or embarking on your first writing journey, this book is designed to be your ultimate guide to transforming your manuscript into a polished document using MS (Microsoft) Word.

Over the years, manuscripts can become cluttered with various formatting issues: extra lines, inconsistent punctuation, unwanted special characters, and irregular line breaks. If you've been writing in MS Word, you've likely encountered some of these challenges. Additionally, the process of preparing a manuscript for submission to an agent or for formatting for publication, whether as an eBook or a physical book, requires careful attention to detail and consistency. *Polished Pages* is here to help you navigate these challenges with ease and confidence.

I've been formatting books for publication for over 30 years. It all started for me way back in my Air Force and corporate days. And boy, oh boy, does the U.S. military love their documentation. Anyway, how we use word processors hasn't really changed much. Bottom line, you have to keep it clean from the beginning, but if you haven't, the checklists in this book will clean up your manuscript with no need to pay someone an arm and a leg to do it for you. Plus, it will save you a little embarrassment with agents.

Why This Book?

MS Word is a powerful tool for writers, offering a wide range of features to help create and format documents. However, its complexity can make it overwhelming—especially for beginners or those who struggle with technology. Many writers find themselves frustrated by unintended formatting errors, hidden characters, or inconsistent styles that can clutter a manuscript and make it difficult to format for publication.

This book is designed specifically for beginners who may not be familiar with MS Word's advanced features. But those highly familiar with MS Word will also find the checklists helpful. The step-by-step checklists provide a clear, structured approach to cleaning up your manuscript, even if you're not comfortable navigating all of MS Word's settings. Each section breaks down common formatting issues and offers easy-to-follow solutions so you can ensure your manuscript is polished and professional without needing advanced technical skills.

By the end of this journey, your manuscript will be clean, consistent, and properly formatted—ready for submission to an agent, editor, or book formatter. Whether you're preparing your work for eBook or print, the techniques in this book will help you meet the industry's professional formatting standards while saving you time, frustration, and unnecessary expenses.

How to Use This Book

This book is structured as a step-by-step checklist to guide you through the manuscript cleanup process. You can use it as a reference to address specific issues as they arise or follow it sequentially for a thorough overhaul of your manuscript. Each chapter focuses on a different aspect of manuscript preparation, providing detailed instructions, practical examples, and valuable tips for avoiding common pitfalls.

Feel free to work through the checklists at your own pace and revisit sections as needed. By the end of this process, you'll have a manuscript that not only meets but exceeds the standards for publication.

The Value of a Clean Manuscript

A clean, well-formatted manuscript is crucial for readability. Clear, consistent formatting enhances the readability of your manuscript, making it easier for editors, beta readers, and ultimately, your audience to engage with your work.

A professionally formatted manuscript reflects your attention to detail and commitment to quality. It demonstrates to publishers and readers alike that you take your work seriously.

Working with a clean manuscript saves you time while you write. When your document is free from unnecessary clutter and inconsistencies, you can focus more on content and less on correcting formatting issues. This streamlined workflow means fewer distractions, allowing you to maintain your creative momentum. Additionally, a clean manuscript makes it easier to spot and address substantive issues during editing, ensuring that your revisions are effective and comprehensive.

Whether you're self-publishing or submitting to a traditional publisher, a clean manuscript simplifies the conversion process to various formats such as an EPUB or PDF, reducing the risk of errors and formatting issues in the final product.

What You'll Learn

The checklists in this book will cover the following key areas:

Formatting Cleanup

Learn how to identify and eliminate extra spaces, lines, and other unwanted formatting that disrupts the flow of your text. You'll delve into techniques for maintaining consistent punctuation and managing special characters that may have crept into your document.

Creating and Applying Styles

Discover how to apply styles in MS Word to ensure a uniform and professional look throughout your manuscript. Styles are essential for consistent formatting and ease of navigation, especially when preparing your work for publication.

Troubleshooting Common Issues

Gain practical advice on resolving common formatting problems that can arise in MS Word. Troubleshooting covers solutions for dealing with hidden characters, unexpected line breaks, and other issues that can complicate the presentation of your manuscript and interfere with the formatting process.

Let's Get Started!

Your manuscript is more than just words on a page; it's a reflection of your creativity and passion for writing. By investing time in cleaning up and formatting your manuscript, you're taking an important step toward presenting your work in the best possible light.

As we embark on this journey together, remember that *Polished Pages* is flexible and adaptable to your needs. Whether you're preparing your manuscript for self-publishing or aiming for traditional publication, this book will equip you with the tools and knowledge to achieve a polished, professional result.

IMPORTANT: If you encounter issues that the checklists don't resolve or your questions are not answered in this book, go to armlinhouse.com/book-formatting and fill out the form, adding the details about your issue. We will get back to you as soon as we can with answers.

Now, let's dive in and transform your manuscript into the masterpiece it's destined to be. Welcome to *Polished Pages*—your guide to perfecting your manuscript in MS Word.

Getting Started with MS Word

Chapter 1

IN THIS CHAPTER, you will set the foundation for your manuscript cleanup journey by configuring your workspace in MS Word. Properly setting up your environment helps make the editing process more efficient. We'll explore how to customize your workspace, activate features like formatting marks, understand key formatting options, and standardize your document's text style.

Setting Up Your Workspace

A well-organized workspace in MS Word significantly enhances your productivity. Start by opening a document that contains text—preferably the manuscript that already contains formatting issues—so you can follow along, setting up your workspace and later cleaning your manuscript.

It's helpful to understand the layout and terminology used in MS Word. Knowing where to find tools—regardless of whether you're using Windows or Mac—will make the process much smoother. So, let's move on to optimizing your environment before diving into the cleanup process.

Menus vs Tabs

One noticeable difference between MS Word on Windows and Mac is the Menu Bar that only appears on Mac when you hover over the very top of the screen. This Menu Bar includes options like File, Edit, View, Insert, and Format. Tabs are available on both Windows and Mac just above the Ribbon, discussed in the next section. The options include Home for text formatting, Layout for page setup, and more. Know that the Menu Bar on Mac includes some of the same tools available on Tabs but may be organized differently. However, some tab features on Windows are only accessible on Mac through the Menu Bar.

Ribbon, Tabs, and Groups

The Ribbon is the toolbar at the top of your MS Word window. It changes based on the Tab option selected and provides quick access to essential Commands and tools. The Font and Paragraph Groups on the Home Tab are shown in the image below.

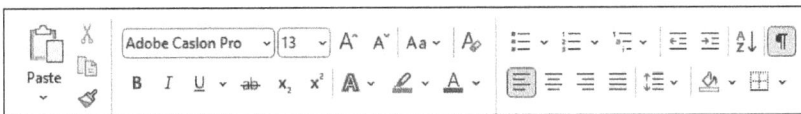

There are several commands used throughout this book to help you clean up your manuscript—some are already visible on the Ribbon, while others may need to be added. In this section, you'll locate the commands you'll use most often, and if any are missing, you'll learn how to add them later. As you progress, you'll also learn what each of these commands does and how it contributes to a cleaner, more professional manuscript.

Let's start with the Commands on the Home Tab's Ribbon, the first options available when you open a document. If you're not already there, above the Ribbon, click on Home and you'll see Commands to change the way text displays.

Notice that the Commands are separated into Groups that are divided by vertical lines. The way the Groups work is another noticeable difference between Windows and Mac. In the Windows version of MS Word, many Groups include a Dialog Box Launcher—a small diagonal arrow in the bottom-right corner of the Group. Clicking this arrow opens a dialog box with more detailed settings. For example, in the Font Group, it opens the Font dialog box. However, this arrow does not appear in the Mac version of MS Word. To access the same advanced settings on a Mac, you'll need to use the Menu Bar at the top of the screen to open dialog boxes.

Now that you understand how to access Commands in the Ribbon—and how they differ slightly between Windows and Mac—you're ready to explore the individual Groups that control key formatting elements. We'll begin with the Paragraph Group, which contains essential tools for adjusting alignment, spacing, indentation, as well as revealing hidden formatting marks that are critical during manuscript cleanup.

The Paragraph Group & Formatting Marks

Consistent paragraph formatting is essential for a clean and professional manuscript. Formatting marks and other symbols are invaluable when cleaning up your manuscript. They reveal non-printing characters that can affect your document's layout and flow. The Command to turn on formatting marks is the paragraph symbol icon in the Paragraph Group as shown in the next image.

1. To turn on formatting marks, click on the ¶ symbol so that it is gray and selected. Alternatively, use the Keyboard Shortcut CTRL + SHIFT + 8 (Windows) or CMD + 8 (Mac) to toggle between activating and deactivating the Command.

2. Notice how the paragraph breaks, spaces, tab marks, and other hidden characters display within the document. We will discuss what each formatting mark represents later. For now, your document will look like the image below.

NOTE: Keep formatting marks visible while cleaning your manuscript—they reveal hidden issues like extra spaces, line breaks, and paragraph returns that need to be removed.

Also, in the Paragraph Group, there are options to adjust alignment, indentation, line spacing, bullets or numbering, and more. You won't use these options because you will manage a paragraph's appearance in Styles, which are covered in a later chapter.

The Font Group

The Commands in the Font Group, shown below, allow you to modify the appearance of your text by adjusting the font type, size, and color. It also contains effects like bolding, italics, and underlining. While you may already be familiar with using these options for basic formatting, they'll still come in handy for applying specific font effects as needed. However, for consistency and efficiency, you'll learn how to set the font type and size through Styles in a later chapter.

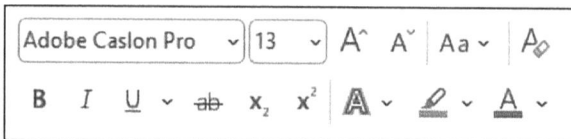

The Styles Group

Speaking of Styles, this Group on the Home Tab, as shown in the image at the top of the next page, is a powerful feature for applying consistent formatting throughout your document.

Heading 4	Normal	Section Break	**Strong**	

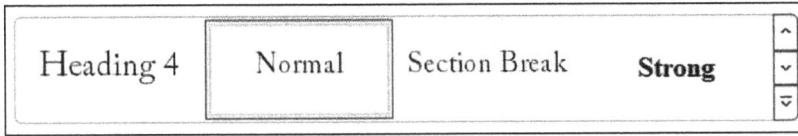

As I continue to mention, there is an entire chapter on styles later in this book, but for now, just know they allow you to format text using predefined settings for headings, body text, bullets, and more. This eliminates the need to manually adjust each instance of formatting—like changing the font and size every time you start a new chapter. Styles are essential for creating a professional, well-structured manuscript. They also support easy navigation and automatic generation of a table of contents, making it simpler for you and your readers to find key sections.

The Editing Group & Find and Replace

The Editing Group is available only in the Windows version of MS Word. Its primary purpose is to provide quick access to search options. These commands allow you to locate and correct formatting inconsistencies, punctuation issues, and special characters across your manuscript. On a Mac, these options are accessed through the Menu Bar or Keyboard Shortcuts.

The most powerful version of this feature is called Advanced Find and Replace, which opens a dialog box containing search settings beyond a simple text search. With it, you can search for formatting, symbols, caret codes, and invisible characters like paragraph marks, tabs, or non-breaking spaces. It's an essential tool for manuscript cleanup.

Because the process for accessing these features is completely different on Windows and Mac, refer to the platform-specific instructions in the next sections.

Windows: Access Find and Replace

🔍 Find ⌄
ᵇ Replace
↳ Select ⌄
Editing

The Editing Group on the Home Tab contains the Find, Replace, and Select options as shown to the left. There are two main ways to access the Advanced Find and Replace dialog box.

- In the Editing Group, click Find to open the Navigation Pane or Replace to open the Advanced Find and Replace dialog box.

- Hit CTRL + H to open the Advanced Find and Replace dialog box.

Mac: Access Find and Replace

Access Find and Replace through the Menu Bar or Keyboard Shortcuts.

- Choose the Menu Bar options Edit > Find > Advanced Find and Replace to open the dialog box.

There is no quick Keyboard Shortcut on Mac that opens Advanced Find and Replace, but you can get there using these instructions:

1. Hit CMD + F to open a field for a simple search.

2. Click on ... to open the menu, then choose Replace to open Find and Replace in the left column.

3. Click on the Settings Gear, then choose Advanced Find and Replace.

4. Click on the Replace Tab, then pull down the arrow to open the advance settings.

Customizing the Ribbon

Up to this point, we've discussed all the Groups needed to clean up a manuscript. While most of the Groups are on default Tabs on the Ribbon, there's a chance one or more might be missing. Or maybe you'd like to add other Commands we haven't discussed. Again, the process for customizing the Ribbon in MS Word differs between Windows and Mac, so follow the instructions that apply to your computer if you need to add any Commands.

Windows: Customize the Ribbon

Start the Ribbon customization through a pop-up menu. Follow these steps for the easiest way to customize the Ribbon on a Windows computer.

1. Right-click anywhere on the Ribbon, then select Customize the Ribbon as shown in the image below.

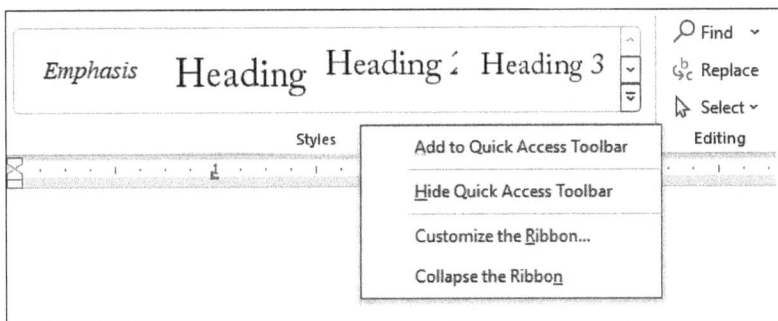

2. Find any of the missing or desired Commands in the Choose Commands From section and add them to the Tabs and Groups where they best belong in the Customize the Ribbon section.

3. Click OK.

Mac: Customize the Ribbon

Customize the Ribbon through preference settings.

1. Hover over the top of the screen to bring up the Menu Bar.

2. Choose Word > Preferences.

3. Under Authoring and Proofing Tools, choose Ribbon & Toolbar.

4. Find any of the missing or desired Commands in the Choose Commands From section and add them to the Tabs and Groups where they best belong in the Customize the Ribbon section.

5. Click Save.

IMPORTANT: Whether you're on Windows or Mac, you'll find quite a few options to add to Tabs and Groups, as well as renaming options for the Commands. Reconfigure options as you like, but the rest of this book will refer to Tabs, Groups, and Commands in default locations. So, changing the locations and names could cause confusion in later checklists.

Disappearing Ribbon

It's possible to minimize the Ribbon to provide more workspace, but sometimes it just seems to disappear. If this happens, don't worry; it's easy to bring it back. However, this is another process that differs between Windows and Mac.

Windows: Restore the Ribbon

Here are the easiest ways to restore the Ribbon:

- Press CTRL + F1 to toggle the Ribbon on or off.

- Double-click any Tab (e.g., Home, Insert, Layout) while the Ribbon is hidden.

Mac: Restore the Ribbon

Here are the easiest ways to restore the Ribbon:

- Press CMD + OPT + R

- Click View in the top menu bar and select Ribbon to toggle it back on.

Yes, there are other ways to pin and collapse the ribbon. Consult MS Word Help or AI for instructions.

Quick Access Toolbar

The Quick Access Toolbar, above the Ribbon and Tabs, provides shortcuts to frequently used Commands. Here you will set up the toolbar with helpful options that may be missing. In the checklists in this book, you will mainly use the Save and Undo/Redo options, but knowing how to customize this toolbar will be helpful for future use.

1. Make sure your toolbar looks like the one above. If it doesn't, click the pull-down arrow beside the toolbar on Windows or the ellipsis (...) on Mac.

2. Check any of the following that are not selected and active:

- Automatically Save
- Open (Windows) or Home (Mac)
- Save
- Undo
- Redo
- Print Preview and Print (Windows) or Print (Mac)

NOTE: At the bottom of the menu, choose More Commands to add additional options not in the pull-down menu. This opens the same dialog box used to customize the Ribbon. Again, cluttering up the toolbar could cause confusion when completing the checklists in this book.

Navigation Pane

The Navigation Pane (shown right) is an excellent tool for navigating your document, especially if your manuscript is lengthy and contains quite a few sections. It provides an easy way to move around via headings, pages, and search results without endless scrolling. Activating and effectively using the Navigation Pane significantly enhance your productivity and streamlines the editing process.

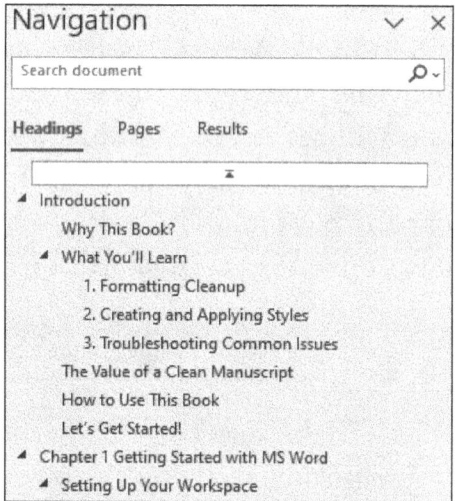

Navigation ∨ ✕

Search document 🔍⌄

Headings   Pages   Results

▲ Introduction
  Why This Book?
  ▲ What You'll Learn
    1. Formatting Cleanup
    2. Creating and Applying Styles
    3. Troubleshooting Common Issues
    The Value of a Clean Manuscript
    How to Use This Book
    Let's Get Started!
▲ Chapter 1 Getting Started with MS Word
  ▲ Setting Up Your Workspace

There are a few easy ways to open the Navigation Pane depending on your type of computer:

- On both Windows and Mac, go to the View Tab on the Ribbon and check the Navigation Pane box in the Show Group.

- On Windows, if the Navigation Pane is closed, use the Keyboard Shortcut CTRL + F to open it directly.

- On Windows, as mentioned in the Find and Replace checklist, selecting Find from the Edit Group opens the Navigation Pane.

Notice there are three tabs, labeled with text on Windows and represented with images on Mac. These tools not only facilitate better navigation and organization; they help maintain a clear overview of your manuscript. More specifically, here's what each section provides:

Headings: This view is useful if you have structured your document using heading styles (e.g., Heading 1, Heading 2, etc.). It displays a collapsible list of all the headings in your document, allowing you to jump to any section with a single click.

Pages: This view shows thumbnail previews of each page in your document. This visual representation makes it easy to navigate through your document by clicking on the desired page's thumbnail. It's especially useful for quickly locating a specific page or verifying the layout of your manuscript.

Results: This view displays all instances of a search term found within your document. Enter a word or phrase in the search box at the top of the Navigation Pane, and the Results view will list all occurrences found, highlighting them within the text. Clicking on a search result takes you directly to its location in the document, making it efficient to review and edit repeated elements or verify consistency.

Revisions (Mac Only): This Tab helps track and manage changes in your document. It displays all comments, edits, and tracked changes in an organized list, making it easy to review modifications without scrolling through the entire document.

Document View

Setting up your document view is an essential step in preparing your manuscript for efficient editing and formatting. By selecting the appropriate layout and adjusting the zoom level, you create a more productive workspace that enhances your ability to focus on the content in your manuscript. Here's how to optimize your document view in MS Word.

Print Layout

Print Layout is particularly useful for catching issues with spacing, alignment, and overall document structure that might not be as apparent in other views.

1. Click on the View Tab, then choose Print Layout in the View Group.

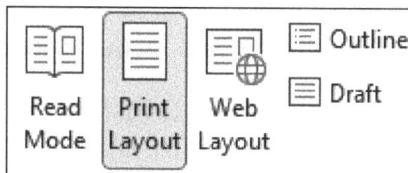

This view provides a realistic representation of your text on a standard page, including margins, page breaks, headers/footers, and spacing.

Zoom Level

Adjusting the Zoom level for comfortable reading and editing is crucial for reducing eye strain and maintaining focus during long editing sessions. A zoom level of 100% or Page Width is usually ideal for most users, as it provides a clear and detailed view of your text without excessive scrolling or strain. But if the text is too small or too large, there are two quick ways to adjust the zoom level as provided below:

- To adjust the zoom level, locate the Zoom control at the bottom-right. Drag the slider to increase or decrease the zoom level. Or click on the percentage box to enter a specific zoom level.

- Alternatively, go to the View Tab and use the Zoom Group to select predefined zoom options like 100%, One Page, Multiple Pages, or Page Width. Click on Zoom for more control over the size of content on the page.

With your MS Word workspace now fully customized and optimized, you are well-prepared to begin the detailed work of cleaning up your manuscript. A well-organized environment not only enhances your productivity but also ensures that you can focus more on the content and less on navigating the software. As you move forward, these initial steps will help streamline your workflow, making the task of cleaning up your manuscript more manageable and less daunting.

Preparing the Manuscript for Cleaning

Chapter 2

BEFORE STARTING THE detailed cleanup, let's make sure your manuscript is in the right format and properly organized. This chapter will show you how to convert your manuscript to MS Word if it was written in another word processor. You will also create a backup file, remove unnecessary content, and standardize the text style. Taking care of these basics now will make the cleanup process in the next chapters faster, easier, and far more effective.

Converting to MS Word

If your manuscript is already an MS Word document, skip this section and move ahead to *Backing Up Your Manuscript*. If you originally wrote your manuscript in another application besides MS Word and want to clean it up using the checklists in this book, you will first convert it to MS Word.

1. Open your manuscript in the word processor you wrote it in, then save or export it as an MS Word document.

NOTE: Most writing applications include a conversion or export option under the File menu, allowing you to save your manuscript in MS Word (.docx) format.

Here are a few common word processors and how to convert to MS Word:

Apple Pages: Use the File > Export option and select to save as an MS Word document.

Scrivener: Use the File > Export option and select to save as an MS Word document. Books within Scrivener are usually in multiple sections, so check the Scrivener Help if the entire manuscript does not export.

Google Docs: Use the File > Download > MS Word (.docx) option to save the manuscript as an MS Word document.

PDF: To convert from PDF, you will need Adobe's Reader or another app that allows you to convert to MS Word.

Otherwise, if you are using a different word processor and don't know how to convert the file to MS Word, a quick Google search or AI inquiry will help you convert the manuscript file. Checking Help in the other word processor is another option for finding instructions.

2. Save the file in the same folder where you store your manuscript so that it doesn't get lost.

Backing Up Your Manuscript

It's important to always keep the original manuscript in case you need to roll back to it. This is because any number of things can happen, so save yourself some time.

In this section, there are two ways to create a copy of your original manuscript. Follow either the *Saving a Backup Copy* or *Copying a File in File Explorer or Finder* checklist in the next sections.

IMPORTANT: You need the entire manuscript in one file, so if you have chapters, sections, or other content in other files, create one file and save it before moving on.

Also note that the steps in the remainder of this section are very basic. If you already know how to create a backup, do it now and consider naming your manuscript backup per the conventions in #4 in the next section below. Then move ahead to Removing Unneeded Content.

Saving a Backup Copy

Use this method to save a copy of your manuscript. The process is similar whether you're using Windows or Mac.

1. Open the complete manuscript in MS Word format if it's not already open.

2. Choose File > Save As (Windows) or Save a Copy (Mac).

3. Find a location to save the copy. Where you stored the original file is a good option, so you have easy access to all file versions later.

4. Save the manuscript copy with a descriptive name such as the title of the work with "CLEANED" at the end. See the example below for help with the filename.

TheGreatGatsby-CLEANED.docx

This file is the one you will clean up using the checklists in this book.

5. Keep the newly copied file open and move on to *Removing Unneeded Content*.

Copying a File in File Explorer or Finder

Here is another way to copy a file in Windows' File Explorer or Mac's Finder, which are file management applications. Just in case you are unfamiliar with either, it's where you access and organize files and folders. It's also where you perform tasks such as copying, moving, renaming, and deleting files.

1. Open File Explorer or Finder and go to the folder where the original manuscript resides.

NOTE: Open File Explorer by clicking on the file folder icon in the taskbar at the bottom in Windows. Finder is the blue icon with the smiley face in the taskbar on a Mac.

---

2. Click on the original file to highlight it.

3. Hit CTRL + C (Windows) or CMD + C (Mac), then hit CTRL + V (Windows) or CMD + V (Mac) to paste a copy of the manuscript. The copied file will have the text "– Copy" at the end of the filename or just "Copy."

4. Right-click on the copy of the manuscript, then choose Rename.

5. Keep the book title at the beginning of the filename and change "Copy" to CLEANED or -CLEANED at the end of the name as shown below.

TheGreatGatsby-CLEANED.docx

6. Hit ENTER (Windows) or RETURN (Mac) to save the change to the new name.

Removing Unneeded Content

Before delving into the detailed cleanup, it's important to remove any content that is not needed, such as the comments and tracked changes. So, in each subsequent section, decide which content to remove based on the final manuscript you need. For example, if you are submitting your manuscript to an agent, you will likely need to keep the title page and header/footer. If you are preparing your manuscript for a book designer to format an eBook or paperback, you will need to remove all content except the actual manuscript.

IMPORTANT: Completing all checklists in this chapter will give you a stripped-down manuscript that's fully prepped for book formatting. Only follow the checklists that apply to your manuscript—there's no need to complete steps that aren't relevant to your formatting goals.

Removing the Title Page

Removing the title page isn't always as easy as deleting the text. This is because most title pages are set up in a separate section with a different first page that doesn't include a header and footer like the rest of the document. When you highlight and delete the content on the title page, the content on the next page moves into the title page section. You could end up with the first page of the first chapter missing a header and footer, while the rest of the document contains them. So, here you will delete the title page content and change the layout setting back to default for the first page.

1. Open the manuscript in MS Word if it's not already open.

2. Go to the first page and turn on paragraph formatting marks if they're not already on. (See *The Paragraph Group & Formatting Marks* in Chapter 1 for instructions.)

3. Remove all content on the title page, including the Section Break. The content from the second page will now appear on the first page, but without the header and footer.

Because the process to remove a different first page is not the same on Windows and Mac, move on to the section you need.

Windows: Reset the First Page Setting

Here's how to restore the first page settings:

1. Go to the Layout Tab and in the Page Setup Group, click on the dialog box launcher.

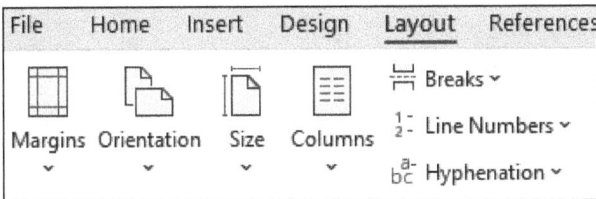

2. Go to the Layout tab and uncheck Different First Page.

3. Click on OK, then save the changes.

Mac: Reset the First Page Setting

Here's how to restore the first page settings:

1. Choose File > Page Setup.

2. Pull down Microsoft Word and change Apply Page Setup Setting To field to Whole Document.

3. Click on OK, then save the changes.

After completing the steps on Windows or Mac, the header and footer in the next section of the document will also display on the first page.

Removing the Header and Footer

Here you will remove the header and footer. Again, only remove it if needed.

1. Double-click on the header if there is text within it. This opens the header/footer view.

2. Remove all text from the header.

3. Page down to the footer and remove any text.

4. Double-click on the main manuscript section to exit the header/footer view.

5. Save the changes.

Removing Comments & Tracked Changes

Before proceeding with the detailed cleanup of your manuscript, it is crucial to remove any comments and tracked changes within the document. Comments and tracked changes can clutter your manuscript, making it difficult to read during the editing process. Removing these elements ensures your manuscript is clean and free from unnecessary annotations, allowing you to focus on the content and formatting without interruptions. This step also helps to maintain a professional appearance, especially if you are sharing your document with editors or beta readers.

Deleting Comments

If you have a document filled with comments, there is one easy way to remove them all. This section will help you get rid of all of them with a few clicks of the mouse.

IMPORTANT: If you don't have an extra original copy of your manuscript, go to the Backing Up Your Manuscript instructions at the beginning of this chapter and create a backup now. Otherwise, all the comments you might need at a future date could be gone.

---

1. Click on the Review Tab and go to the Comments Group as shown below. It looks a little different between Windows and Mac, but the options are mostly the same.

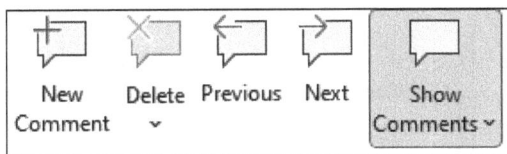

2. Click on Show Comments if it's not gray or active. Any comments in your document will display on the right side and will look similar to what is shown below.

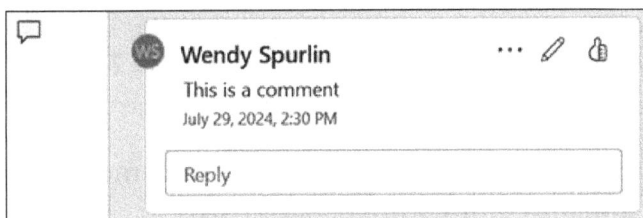

NOTE: If comments are not on, you will only see small bubbles in the right margin. If comments are on, you will see the complete comment.

---

3. Take one last minute to page through the comments and make sure you won't lose anything important when you delete all comments.

4. In the Comments Group, click on the arrow for the Delete Command. The image below is from Windows. On a Mac, the arrow is beside the Delete Command.

WARNING: When you complete the next step, there is no alert that all comments will be deleted. If you remove them by mistake, use the Undo command—CTRL + Z (Windows) or CMD + Z (Mac)—to bring them back. You can also use the Undo/Redo buttons in the Quick Access Toolbar.

---

5. Choose Delete All Comments in Document and you will have a manuscript without comments.

6. Save the changes.

Applying or Rejecting Tracked Changes

Tracked changes can obscure the true state of your manuscript, making it difficult to accurately assess the text. Addressing tracked changes here helps maintain clarity and prevents potential confusion during subsequent cleanup stages.

IMPORTANT: Yes, I'm warning you again. If you don't have an extra original copy of your manuscript, go to the Backing Up Your Manuscript instructions at the beginning of this chapter and create a backup now. Otherwise, all the tracked changes will be lost.

---

1. Click on the Review Tab to open its Ribbon and find the Markup Group as shown below on Windows. This section looks similar on a Mac.

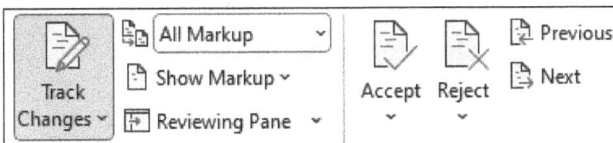

2. If you're not seeing any tracked changes, click on Track Changes to activate them. Make sure Track Changes is gray and All Markup is selected as shown in the previous image.

NOTE: When Track Changes is turned on, a summary of all changes appears in the right margin. The modified text is also in color and possibly underlined within the document to show what has been added, deleted, or altered.

---

3. Decide if you would like to accept or reject tracked changes all at once or walk through accepting and rejecting each of the tracked changes. Complete one of the following options based on your preference.

WARNING: Like comments, when you accept or reject all tracked changes at once, there is no alert that the changes are being made. If you accept or reject them all by mistake, use the Undo command—CTRL + Z (Windows) or CMD + Z (Mac)—to bring them back. You can also use the Undo/Redo buttons in the Quick Access Toolbar.

If you want to accept or reject changes all at once, open the menu for Accept or Reject and choose Accept All Changes or Reject All Changes.

If you want to walk through the changes, position the cursor within the document, then click on Accept or Reject to highlight the next change. Click on Accept or Reject again to accept or reject the change. Continue walking through the changes, accepting and rejecting until a message displays, telling you that there are no more changes, as shown below.

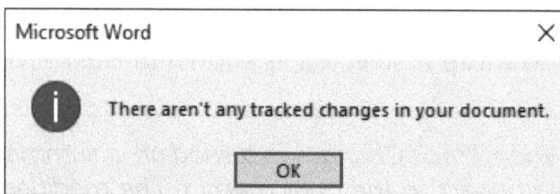

Microsoft Word ×

There aren't any tracked changes in your document.

OK

4. Click OK if you were walking though changes, then save the changes.

Applying the Normal Paragraph Style

In this section, you'll apply the Normal paragraph style to all text in your manuscript to create a consistent foundation before cleanup. This step is essential because manuscripts often contain inconsistent formatting—like headers with different font sizes or spacing—especially after years of editing. Applying a single base style eliminates those variations. The font assigned will be the default Normal style, but don't worry—you'll customize it in a later chapter if needed.

IMPORTANT: If you're already familiar with styles and confident they're correctly applied throughout your manuscript, you can skip this section. However, if you've copied and pasted content from other sources, the text may appear styled correctly when it's not. Reapplying the style might suddenly change the formatting—revealing underlying inconsistencies. That's why it's always a good idea to start fresh and reassign styles to ensure a clean, consistent manuscript.

Select All Text

In this step, you will select all text in the manuscript. Because this is done differently on Windows and Mac, go to the section based on your computer type.

Windows: Select All

Follow these instructions to select all text.

1. Go to the Home Tab if it's not open, then to the Editing Group.

2. Click on Select to open the menu as shown below.

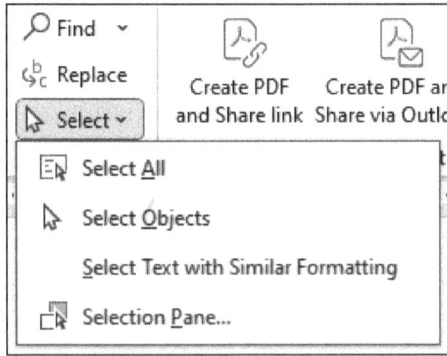

3. Choose Select All to select all the text in the manuscript.

Mac: Select All

Follow these instructions to select all text.

1. Go to the top menu bar and select Edit > Select All.

NOTE: If you'd rather use a Keyboard Shortcut, hit CTRL + A (Windows) or CMD + A (Mac) to select all text.

Apply the Normal Paragraph Style

In this step, you will apply the Normal text style to all text. When you do this, your text may look unformatted and messy. Don't worry. The following chapters will clean up the text. But if you run into any bizarre formatting issues not covered in this book, go to https://armlinhouse.com/book-formatting and explain your issue, and we'll help you resolve the problem.

1. On the Home Tab, in the Styles Group, click on the Normal text style.

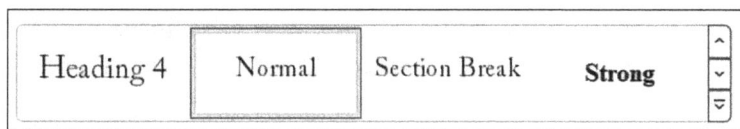

Heading 4	Normal	Section Break	**Strong**

If you don't see the Normal text style listed, use the arrows to page through the styles, or open the Styles Group to find Normal. If you still can't find the Normal style, see *Styles Missing from the Styles Group* in Chapter 5.

2. Page through the manuscript and make sure all text looks consistent. It's okay to have bolded and italicized text, but text should not display in variable size and font type.

NOTE: Sometimes formatting inconsistencies—like random bold text, varying font sizes, or leftover styling from pasted content—can remain even after applying the Normal style. In those cases, clearing all formatting removes any manual overrides and resets the text completely. If everything already looks uniform, you can skip the step in the next paragraph. But when in doubt, clearing formatting ensures you're starting with a truly clean slate.

If the text is in particularly inconsistent shape, select all text again (if it's no longer selected), then click Clear All Formatting in the Font group. After that, reapply the Normal paragraph style. **Be careful, though—using this command removes all formatting, including italics and bold, so use it only if necessary.**

REMINDER: If the results look wrong or messy, you can always undo the changes. In some cases, it may be easier to complete the cleanup steps in Chapters 3 and 4 first before applying the Normal style. And in Chapter 5, you'll get additional help with standardizing text using styles.

---

3. Save the changes.

Shortcut Keys for Special Characters

Before starting the cleanup in the next two chapters, it's helpful to know a few Shortcut Keys that insert special characters quickly. These shortcuts save time and ensure consistency, especially when dealing with non-breaking spaces and punctuation like em dashes and ellipses. MS Word supports several built-in shortcuts that work differently on Windows and Mac.

Here is a limited list of commonly used characters and their Shortcut Keys that you will use in later checklists:

Windows: Shortcut Keys

Non-Breaking Space: CTRL + SHIFT + SPACE

Em Dash (—): CTRL + ALT + - (numeric keypad)

En Dash (–): CTRL + - (numeric keypad)

Ellipsis (…): CTRL + ALT + Period (.)

Mac: Shortcut Keys

Em Dash (—): SHIFT + OPT + Hyphen (-)

En Dash (–): OPT + Hyphen (-)

Ellipsis (…): OPT + Semicolon (;)

Inserting Special Characters

You can also insert characters from the Symbol dialog box, from the Special Characters Tab.

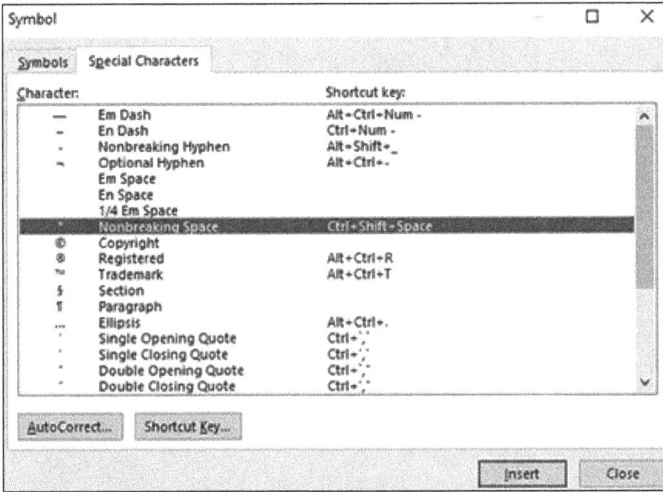

There are more characters and symbols available as shown in the image above. Here's how to insert these characters.

1. Place the cursor where you need the character or symbol.

2. Click on the Insert Tab and go to the Symbols Group on the far right.

3. Click Symbol (Windows) or Advanced Symbol (Mac). If you are on Mac, the symbol library opens. If you are on Windows, select More Symbols to open the Symbol Library.

4. Click on the Special Characters Tab.

5. Find the Character you need and highlight it.

6. Click Insert and the symbol appears where you placed the cursor.

While this will be a helpful checklist to refer to later, the Short-cut Keys are also in other checklists where you will need them.

By standardizing the text style, removing unneeded text, and resolving comments and tracked changes, you've created a starting point to brush up your manuscript. With this streamlined foundation, you can focus on refining content and polishing the presentation more efficiently.

Removing Sections, Breaks & Spaces

Chapter 3

BEFORE SUBMITTING YOUR manuscript to an agent, editor, or book formatter, it's important to clean up any hidden formatting issues that can make your document appear messy and unprofessional. Extra line breaks, spaces, tabs, and section breaks often accumulate during the writing and editing process—especially if you've copied and pasted text from various sources or switched between word processors. These inconsistencies can disrupt text flow, create unwanted white space, and lead to formatting problems that slow down the next stages of production. This chapter will guide you through the steps to efficiently remove unnecessary sections, breaks, and spaces.

Back in Chapter 1, you turned on Formatting Marks by clicking on the Paragraph Symbol in the Paragraph Group on the Home Tab. If you've turned it off and don't see any symbols within the text, turn it back on before completing the checklists in this chapter. When formatting marks are on, your manuscript will look like the sample document on the next page. We'll discuss what each symbol represents in the applicable sections where they are cleaned up.

Viewing Formatting Marks and other non-printing characters is a vital step in the manuscript cleanup process. By familiarizing yourself with these symbols, you gain a deeper understanding of your document's structure and can identify and correct formatting issues more effectively. This attention to detail not only enhances the appearance of your manuscript but also prepares it for a smoother transition to the next stages of editing and publication.

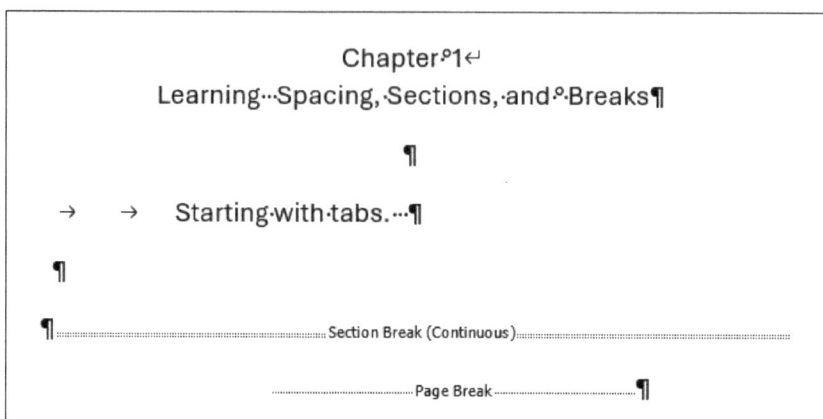

Preparing Find and Replace

Back in Chapter 1, you learned how to open Advanced Find and Replace. As you'll soon see, it is a powerful tool that helps you quickly locate and fix formatting inconsistencies, such as extra line breaks, tabs, and unnecessary spaces. Instead of manually scanning your manuscript, you can use this feature to clean up common issues efficiently and consistently. The steps in this section will guide you through using Advanced Find and Replace to create a more polished, professional manuscript and prepare it for the next stage of editing or formatting.

Here's a refresher on how to open Find and Replace, depending on your computer type.

- On Windows, open the Find and Replace dialog box with CTRL + H.

- On Mac, go to the top menu bar and choose Edit > Find > Advanced Find and Replace.

1. In the Find and Replace dialog, go to the Replace Tab.

2. Click on the More >> button (Windows) or the down arrow button (Mac).

3. Go to the Search Option or Search section and change the Search field to All.

When you're ready to search, the Find and Replace window will look like the dialog box shown below. Again, they look different on Windows and Mac, but they contain the same search options.

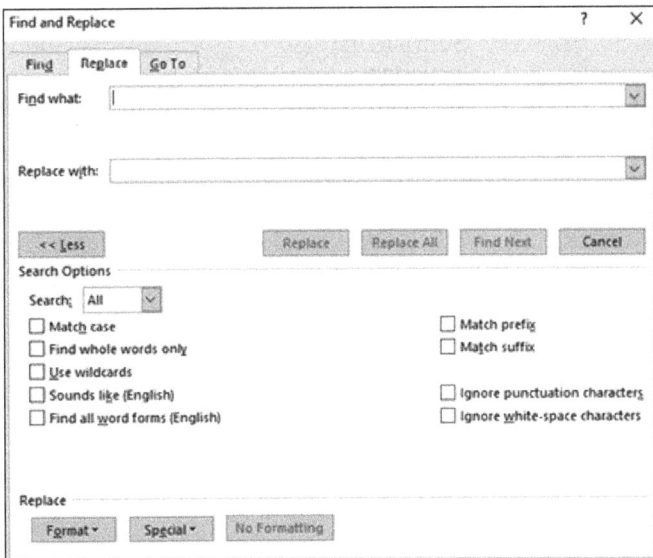

Understanding Caret Codes

Before delving into Find and Replace, it's important to understand caret codes, which allow you to search for and replace formatting symbols, special characters, and non-printing elements in your manuscript. Since many formatting issues—such as extra paragraph marks, manual line breaks, and non-breaking spaces—are invisible in standard view, using caret codes helps you accurately locate and fix them.

Standard Caret Codes

Here are some common caret codes used to represent document formatting. You'll use several of these in the cleanup checklists that follow:

^p	Paragraph Mark
^l	Manual Line Break
^m	Manual Page Break
^b	Section Break
^t	Tab Character
^w	White Space
^s	Non-Breaking Space
^d	Field Code
^n	Column Break
^e	Endnote Mark
^f	Footnote Mark

Notice how these caret codes start with a caret (^) and include a letter or character representing a specific element in your document. They are invaluable for quickly locating and removing formatting issues that are difficult to spot manually. Instead of scrolling through the entire manuscript, you can use caret codes to efficiently clean up your document, saving time and ensuring consistency.

There are other codes, some of which are numeric and represent punctuation, that you will use in the next chapter. Always check if your version of MS Word interprets the code. Some codes work in Find, but not always in Replace, and vice versa So, don't be surprised if a message pops up and says it can't find something, even if you know that the formatting or character exists. There are workarounds for these situations we will cover in the checklists. Until then, let's clean up sections, breaks, and spaces.

Removing Sections, Breaks, and Spaces

You're now ready to remove the formatting issues that cause display problems and unwanted white space in your manuscript. This includes excessive section breaks, page breaks, line breaks, paragraph returns, tabs, spaces, and non-breaking spaces. There is a checklist for each issue.

IMPORTANT: Some checklists—like Removing Manual Page Breaks—include optional steps for removing formatting. While optional, it's strongly recommended that you remove all unnecessary breaks now to start with a clean slate. In the styles chapter, you'll learn how to add white space properly using paragraph settings, without manually inserting page or line breaks.

Removing Section Breaks

Section breaks help organize your manuscript by dividing it into sections with different formatting. While useful for print documents, they can cause unexpected white space or layout issues if misused. The image below shows what a section break looks like. Insert them carefully to maintain a clean, logical structure, especially when preparing your manuscript for different media formats.

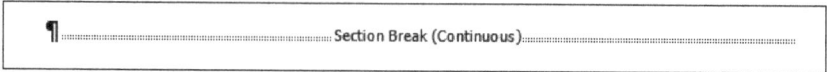

¶ ·····································Section Break (Continuous)·····································

Use this checklist to remove section breaks that are creating unnecessary white space.

1. Place the cursor at the beginning of your manuscript.

2. Go to the Find and Replace dialog box and place the cursor in the Find What field.

3. Go to the Replace section at the bottom of the dialog box and click on Special.

4. Choose Section Break. Notice the caret code ^b is now in the Find What field.

NOTE: *^b is one of the carat codes discussed earlier, and you can type the Command into the Find What field instead of using the menu. This works for any of the breaks you'll search for in this chapter.*

---

5. Leave the Replace With field empty and make sure there are no spaces in the field, otherwise you will remove the section break and add an extra empty space to your manuscript in its place.

6. Click on Find Next to find a section break. Decide if the section break is needed or not. Remember it is best to remove all section breaks unless you are absolutely sure you need it.

7. If it's not needed, click on Replace. If it is, click on Find Next.

If you feel comfortable removing all sections at once, use the Replace All button. If not, continue walking through Find Next and Replace until you reach the end of the document.

IMPORTANT: When you remove some breaks, extra lines sometimes insert into the manuscript. Don't remove them now. You will remove multiple blank lines at once later.

---

8. When the No Results Found message pops up, click OK.

If you replaced all, a summary of changes pops up in a message box. Click OK to close it.

9. Save the changes.

Removing Manual Page Breaks

Page breaks indicate the end of one page by forcing the text after them onto a new page. They are essential for controlling where content is placed, especially in manuscripts where certain sections, chapters, or visual elements must start on their own page.

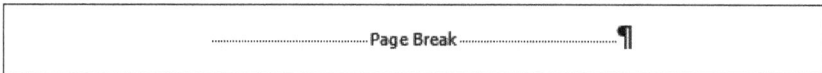

···························Page Break···························¶

Above is an example of a page break. If misused, they can leave large gaps or unnecessary white space in the manuscript, especially if they're inserted manually between sections or chapters. Instead of relying on manual page breaks, it's best to build them into paragraph styles—such as applying a "Page Break Before" setting in your chapter heading style. This ensures consistency across the document and reduces the risk of formatting errors. Follow this checklist to remove unnecessary manual page breaks and prepare your manuscript for cleaner, more professional formatting.

1. Empty the Find What field and place the cursor there.

2. Click on Special in the Find and Replace dialog box, then choose Manual Page Break. Notice the caret code ^m is now in the Find What field.

3. Leave the Replace With field blank and make sure there are no spaces in the field.

4. As you did with section breaks, click on Find Next to find a page break.

5. Click on Replace, then continue walking through Find Next and Replace until you reach the end of the document. When the No Results Found message pops up, click OK.

If you feel comfortable removing all page breaks at once, use the Replace All button. This option provides a summary of the number of replacements. Click OK to close the message.

6. Save the changes.

Removing Manual Line Breaks

A manual line break, also known as a soft return, moves text to the next line without starting a new paragraph. The Keyboard Shortcut SHIFT + ENTER inserts a manual line break. While they are useful in specific scenarios, overusing them can make formatting more difficult, especially if the text is later edited or needs to be converted to a different format. For most situations, it is better to use standard paragraph breaks or styles for proper formatting.

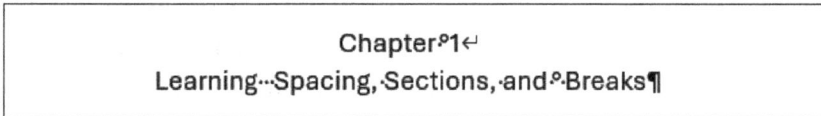

Chapter°1↵
Learning···Spacing,·Sections,·and°·Breaks¶

In the image sample above, there's a manual line break at the end of the first line, beside the number 1. It's represented by a left-shifting arrow. Removing manual line breaks can be tricky because removing them improperly can cause other formatting issues. So, follow this checklist carefully.

1. Empty the Find What field and place the cursor there.

2. Click on Special in the Find and Replace dialog box, then choose Manual Line Break. Notice the caret code ^l (a small letter L) is added to the Find What field.

3. Leave the Replace With field empty, making sure there are no spaces in the field to start.

4. As you did in the previous two checklists, click on Find Next to find a manual line break.

WARNING: Don't use Replace All or you could merge all text into 1 paragraph.

5. Identify the formatting issue using these scenarios, then follow the instructions to remove the manual line break:

- **The break separates a single paragraph with no space between the text on the first line, where the manual break sits and the line below**. In the Replace With field, enter a space using the space bar or enter ^w, then click on Replace. This combines the text back into one standard paragraph with a space between words.

- **The break separates a single paragraph with a space between the text on the first line, where the manual break sits and the line below**. Empty out the Replace With field, then click on Replace. This combines the text back into one standard paragraph.

- **The break separates text into two paragraphs**. Enter ^p in the Replace With field, then click on Replace. This separates the text into two standard paragraphs.

6. Continue searching for manual page breaks and remove them per the scenarios in the previous steps.

NOTE: In this case, it's better to walk through finding each occurrence and manually replacing the breaks. And don't worry if you add additional space accidentally. There is a checklist later in this chapter to remove extra spaces.

---

7. When the No Results Found message pops up, click OK.

8. Save the changes.

Removing Empty Lines or Paragraph Marks

Each time you press the ENTER key, MS Word inserts a paragraph break or mark (¶) at the end of the line. These breaks are also known as the pilcrow symbol. While paragraph breaks are essential for structuring text, inserting them excessively, without content creates unintended white space gaps that leads to formatting issues in your manuscript. Blank lines make the document look sloppy and inconsistent, especially in professionally formatted books.

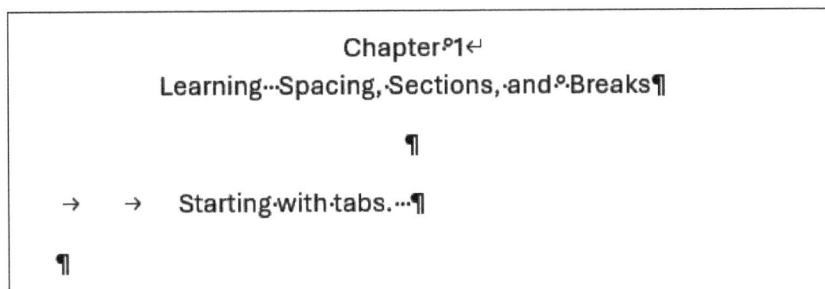

Chapter·1↵
Learning···Spacing,·Sections,·and·ᵖ·Breaks¶

¶

→   →   Starting·with·tabs.···¶

¶

If you want extra white space between paragraphs, set it up using Styles (best option) or adjust the paragraph spacing in the Paragraph settings, rather than relying on paragraph returns. This ensures consistency throughout your manuscript and prevents unnecessary white space when converting the document into an eBook or print-ready format.

In this section, you'll remove empty lines like the ones in the previous image example. It's a good idea to page through the manuscript first to see how many empty lines there are in a row throughout. As you'll see in step 1, if there are multiple empty lines, you'll need to start the search with additional paragraph caret codes.

1. Go to the Find and Replace dialog box, and in the Find What field, enter ^p^p. Or start with more ^p symbols if the manuscript has a lot of blank lines from empty paragraph returns or breaks.

NOTE: ^p represents 1 normal separation between para-graphs. A search with ^p^p only looks for 1 empty line between paragraphs. If you have many empty lines with paragraph marks on pages, start with ^p^p^p or ^p^p^p^p plus.

---

2. In the Replace With section, enter ^p.

3. Click on Replace All, or step through the removal with Find Next and Replace.

4. Make sure all the empty paragraphs have been removed. Run Find and Replace again, as in the previous steps, using the number of needed ^p paragraph caret codes until all extra lines are gone.

5. When the No Results Found message pops up for a ^p^p find, click OK.

6. Save the changes.

Removing Tabs

Arrows pointing to the right represent tab stops within a docu-ment. Tabs are used to align text horizontally and can be useful for creating consistent indents. However, excessive or incon-sistent use of tabs can affect the alignment and layout of your manuscript. This is why it's important to standardize tab usage by using proper indentation styles.

> →　　→　　**Starting·with·tabs.···¶**

One of the most common inconsistencies I see in manuscripts is when writers mix the Normal paragraph style—set up with a first-line indent—with manual formatting, like hitting Enter and then Tab to start a new paragraph. This creates extra, unwanted space—often a full inch—at the beginning of paragraphs. It might sound a little confusing, but the fix is simple. Here's how to remove tabs and clean things up.

1. In the Find What field of the Find and Replace dialog box, enter ^t, or choose Special > Tab Character.

NOTE: ^t represents a tab. This search looks for 1 tab. Similar to empty paragraphs, if tabs are used excessively, you may need to search for multiple tabs.

---

2. In the Replace With section, empty the field of any content or spaces.

3. Click on Replace All, or step through the removal with Find Next and Replace.

4. Run Find and Replace again if needed, to make sure all the tabs have been removed.

5. When the No Results Found message pops up, click OK.

6. Save the changes.

Removing Extra Spaces

Dots between words represent a space, as shown in the example image below. Notice there are many spaces after the period at the end of the sentence that are not needed. These space marks are the most frequently seen symbols in text. Multiple consecutive dots indicate extra spaces, which can disrupt the flow of text and should be removed for a cleaner appearance.

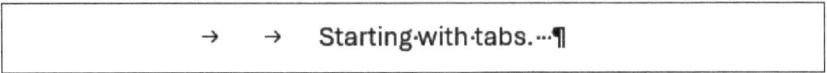

> →   →   Starting·with·tabs.···¶

If you're older, like me, you might remember when it was standard to insert two spaces after sentence-ending punctuation and before starting the next sentence. It's no longer necessary to place two spaces between sentences. In fact, this went out of style a long time ago thanks to all the fonts we now have in word processors vs. typewriters. Still, some of us oldies can't completely kick the habit of adding two spaces. That's why it's a good idea to look for and change double-spaces to single-spaces using the following steps.

1. In the Find and Replace dialog box, in the Find What field, add ^w^w for 2 spaces or choose Special > White Space twice.

NOTE: While ^w represents a space between words, Find and Replace also recognizes the use of the spacebar to enter a normal space. So, you can use the ^w in steps 1 and 2 or use the space bar instead in the Find What and Replace With fields.

2. In Replace With add ^w or 1 space.

3. Click on Replace All, or step through the removal with Find Next and Replace.

4. When the No Results Found message pops up, click OK.

5. Save the changes.

Removing Space at the End of Paragraphs

Extra spaces at the end of a paragraph often happen by accident—or simply out of habit while typing. Even if you've already removed extra spaces using a previous checklist, single spaces at the end of paragraphs may still remain. Removing them helps maintain clean, consistent formatting throughout your manuscript.

1. In the Find what field in the Find and Replace dialog box, enter ^w^p.

NOTE: The caret code ^w represents a single white space, but when combined with ^p, it tells MS Word to find and remove any spaces that appear just before a paragraph break. This helps eliminate stray spaces at the end of paragraphs.

---

2. In the Replace with section, enter ^p.

3. Click on Replace All, or step through the removal with Find Next and Replace.

4. When the No Results Found message pops up, click OK.

5. Save the changes.

Removing Unneeded Non-Breaking Spaces

A non-breaking space prevents the text on either side of it from being separated or wrapped onto a new line. In the image example, there is a non-breaking space, represented by the circle after the word "Chapter" that stops the line from displaying on multiple lines.

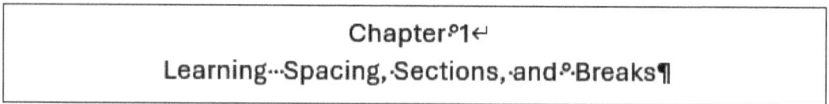

> Chapter°1↵
> Learning···Spacing,·Sections,·and°·Breaks¶

The insertion of these non-printed characters happens frequently during the conversion of a document from one word processor app to MS Word.

While in certain circumstances, a non-breaking space is very helpful, a manuscript can sometimes be littered with them. In most cases, the writer doesn't even know they're there until the formatting marks are turned on. All they see are jagged line breaks with excessive white space and scrunched text. Unless you really need to keep text together, it's best to get rid of all the non-breaking spaces that sneak into your manuscript.

NOTE: If you do want to use one, the Shortcut Keys to insert this Special Character is CTRL + SHIFT + SPACEBAR (Windows) or CMD + SHIFT + SPACEBAR (Mac).

One helpful detail is that using ^w or a blank space in the Find What field also identifies non-breaking spaces. So, when you removed extra spaces earlier, you likely removed extra non-breaking spaces as well. However, single non-breaking spaces may still remain between words, which is why you'll replace them with standard spaces in the next checklist.

1. In the Find What field on the Find and Replace dialog box, enter ^s, or choose Special > Nonbreaking Space.

2. In the Replace With section, enter ^w to replace the nonbreaking space with a regular space. As in the previous checklist, you can also use the space bar to create a standard space in this field.

3. Click on Replace All, or step through the removal with Find Next and Replace.

4. When the No Results Found message pops up, click OK.

5. Save the changes.

Additional Hidden Characters to Watch For

While this chapter has guided you through cleaning up the most common formatting marks, there are a few lesser-known hidden characters and symbols in MS Word that can also impact your manuscript's layout and behavior—especially in longer or older documents.

Object anchors are small anchor symbols that appear when you insert floating elements like images or text boxes. These anchors indicate which paragraph the object is attached to, and if the text around them moves, the object may shift with it. If you're experiencing unexpected image movement, it's worth checking whether an object is anchored to the correct paragraph and adjusting the layout options as needed.

In tables, you may encounter **end-of-cell markers**, which are invisible by default but control formatting within each table cell. Sometimes extra paragraph marks or spacing attached to these markers can interfere with cell alignment or create uneven table structures. Cleaning up hidden content at the end of cells can help restore consistency across your tables.

Column breaks are another hidden element that can disrupt formatting. These are used in multi-column layouts to force text to the next column. While useful in newsletters or brochures, they are rarely needed in book manuscripts. If you converted your manuscript from another template or copied text from formatted sources, column breaks may have come along with it. Removing them can resolve unexpected gaps or white space in your document.

You may also run into **field codes,** which are placeholders for dynamic content like page numbers, dates, or cross-references. These sometimes appear as shaded gray fields or as curly-braced code, such as { PAGE }. You can toggle between viewing field codes and their results by pressing ALT + F9 (Windows) or OPT + F9 (Mac). While they're usually harmless, they can be confusing if you're not expecting them.

Finally, some older documents or tracked changes may contain hidden text, which shows as a dotted underline when visible. This content won't print unless you explicitly enable it, but it can affect layout and word count. To check for hidden text, go to File > Options > Display (Windows) or Word > Preferences > View (Mac) and make sure the Hidden Text option is enabled so you can review and remove it if necessary.

Though these characters are less common, they can still sneak into a manuscript—especially if it's been passed through different programs or heavily edited. Knowing how to recognize and manage them gives you even greater control over your final document and helps ensure a clean, reliable manuscript from start to finish.

By following the steps in this chapter, you've tackled a crucial part of manuscript cleanup—removing unnecessary sections, breaks, spaces, and formatting inconsistencies that can disrupt text flow and cause errors. Using formatting marks and the Find and Replace tool, you've transformed your document into a cleaner, more professional manuscript. Now, let's move on to cleaning up the punctuation.

Standardizing the Punctuation

Chapter 4

CLEANING UP SECTIONS, breaks, and spaces was just the first step in refining your manuscript. Now, it's time to address another common issue—inconsistent punctuation. Variations in dashes, quotation marks, and ellipses can make a book look unprofessional and disrupt the reading experience.

Even with careful writing and editing, punctuation errors creep in. MS Word and other word processors often insert different punctuation styles automatically, resulting in a mix of em dashes and en dashes, straight and curly quotation marks, or ellipses that appear as either three separate periods or a single character. These inconsistencies may seem minor but can cause formatting issues, especially in eBooks, where punctuation can break across lines.

This chapter will help you identify and fix frequently found inconsistencies in punctuation to create a polished, professional manuscript. Standardizing punctuation now will prevent formatting headaches later and keep readers focused on your story.

Caret Codes vs Character Codes

In the previous chapter, you learned that caret codes are a powerful tool in Find and Replace for searching for specific formatting marks, non-printing characters, and symbols. So far, you've used the caret (^) with a letter, but it can also be combined with character codes, which represent specific punctuation, symbols, and special characters. Character codes are based on Unicode or ASCII values assigned to these elements.

To use a character code in Find and Replace, you add a zero before the value (e.g., ^0133 for an ellipsis).

While the checklists in the next section provide the character codes you'll need to clean up punctuation in your manuscript, you can easily find character codes directly within MS Word. Follow these steps to locate the character code for any punctuation or symbol.

1. Click on the Insert Tab and go to the Symbols Group on the far right.

2. Click Symbol (Windows) or Advanced Symbol (Mac). If you are on Mac, the Symbol Library opens. If you are on Windows, select More Symbols to open it.

3. On the Symbols Tab, locate and click on the punctuation or symbol you need a character code for.

4. On Windows only, go to the From pull-down menu at the bottom right and select ASCII (decimal) to view the character code you'll need.

On Mac only, look below the box with the symbols and you'll find the correct character code before the Unicode in the parenthesis.

5. Use the character code in Find and Replace by preceding it with a caret (^) and a zero (0), although not all character codes need the preceding zero. For example, 133 becomes

^0133 to find an ellipsis because it is ASCII. Certain Unicode values such as 33 for an exclamation mark do not require a zero and only needs ^33 for a search.

Confusing enough? As long as you know to try a zero or not, you should be able to find what you're looking for. Yes, this process can be very "trial and error." Don't worry. The character codes you need for a standard cleanup are in the checklists in this book.

Enabling AutoCorrect for Smart Quotes and Punctuation

Enabling Smart Quotes is essential before replacing straight quotation marks. This AutoCorrect setting ensures MS Word inserts the correct left or right quotation marks automatically. Enabling AutoCorrect also lets MS Word convert double dashes (--) into em dashes (—) and three periods (. . .) into a proper ellipsis (…), maintaining consistent punctuation as you type. The next checklist will walk you through enabling these settings before using Find and Replace.

1. Go to File > Options > Proofing (Windows) or Word > Preferences > AutoCorrect (Mac).

2. If you're on Windows, click on the AutoCorrect Options button, then go to the AutoFormat as You Type Tab.

If you are on Mac, you will only need to click on the Auto-Format As You Type Tab.

3. Check the following options:

- "Straight quotes" with "smart quotes"

- Hyphens (--) with dash (—)

4. Go to the AutoCorrect Tab, then go to the Replace Text as You Type section. Make sure autocorrecting and changing three periods to an ellipsis is on the list. If it's not, add it.

5. Click OK, then OK again to save your settings on Windows, or close the window to save the settings on Mac.

Unfortunately, changing the AutoCorrect settings will not fix any issues that are already in your manuscript. Fortunately, the checklists in this chapter will walk you through the process of cleaning up the inconsistent punctuation.

Standardizing Punctuation with Find and Replace

Find and Replace makes it easy to fix punctuation inconsistencies without manually scanning your manuscript. By using character codes in searches, you can quickly standardize quotation marks, dashes, and ellipses in just a few steps.

Open your manuscript with MS Word if it isn't already open, then open Advanced Find and Replace. For instructions, go back to the beginning of Chapter 3 for instructions.

Before making replacements, keep in mind there are three fundamental ways to find and replace inconsistent punctuation.

- Copy a punctuation mark from your manuscript, such as straight quotes, and paste it into the Find/Replace fields.

- Enter character or caret codes (^) in Find/Replace to search for specific punctuation.

- Select punctuation from the Special menu at the bottom of the Find and Replace dialog box, although these options are limited.

Quotation Marks

Word processors often mix straight (" " and ' ') quotation marks with curly (" " and ' ') quotation marks, however, curly quotation marks are the industry standard for publishing. Converting straight quotation marks to Smart Quotes ensures a cleaner, more professional manuscript. Here are the steps to make the change.

1. In Find What, enter ^034 or a straight double quotation mark (").

2. In Replace With, enter ^0147 or a curly double quotation mark (").

3. Click Replace All—MS Word will automatically insert curly quotation marks. Or use Find Next and Replace to walk through the changes.

4. Repeat the process for single quotation marks, entering ^039 or a straight single quotation mark (') in Find What. In Replace With, enter ^0146 or a curly single quotation mark (').

MS Word typically replaces straight quotation marks with the correct left or right curly quotation marks automatically. However, errors can still occur, especially if the document contains copied text from multiple sources or has been edited across different programs. For example, MS Word tends to place a left curly quotation mark after an em dash (—") at the end of a dialog piece. A quick search for em dashes will help you correct this issue.

After converting quotation marks, scan or further search through your text carefully, paying close attention to dialogue and contractions, where errors are most common. If you spot any incorrect quotation marks, manually adjust them to maintain consistency throughout your manuscript. Using Find and Replace can speed up the process, but a final visual check ensures accuracy.

Em Dash & En Dash

Dashes are often inconsistent in manuscripts, especially when different word processors or typing habits introduce variations. As you've seen with AutoCorrect, sometime two hyphens (--) are in place of an em dash (—), while en dashes (–) sometimes appear where an em dash should be.

An em dash (—) and an en dash (–) serve different purposes in writing and should be used correctly for a polished, professional manuscript. The em dash is the longest and is often used in place of commas, parentheses, or colons to create emphasis or indicate an abrupt break in thought. It adds clarity and impact to a sentence without disrupting flow. For example: She wasn't just angry—she was furious. The en dash, slightly shorter than the em dash, is primarily used to show a range (e.g., pages 10–15 or June–August) or to indicate a connection between words of equal importance (e.g., New York–London flight). And, of course, the regular dash, or hyphen (-), is the shortest of the dash types and is primarily used to join words or parts of words. It appears in compound words (well-known author, high-speed chase), hyphenated names (Jean-Paul), and to divide words at the end of a line when space is limited. Using the correct dash ensures consistency and improves readability in your manuscript.

In the following steps, you'll replace double hyphens with proper em dashes and ensure en dashes are used correctly.

1. To search for em dashes that are not properly punctuated, enter double dashes (--) in Find What.

2. In Replace With, enter an actual em dash (—) or enter ^+ (caret code) or ^0151 (character code). You can also select an em dash from the Special Characters pull-down menu at the bottom of the Find and Replace dialog box to insert the ^+ caret code.

REMINDER: Shortcut Keys for an em dash are CTRL + ALT + - NUMERIC KEYPAD (Windows) and SHIFT + OPT + HYPHEN (Mac). See Chapter 2, Shortcut Keys for Special Characters for more information.

---

3. Use Find Next and Replace to walk through the changes, making sure the double dashes are actual em dashes. Hit Replace if you need to change a double dash into an em dash. Otherwise, manually change the double dash into an en dash or single dash based on proper usage.

NOTE: It is not acceptable to keep double dashes in a manuscript. It is only used as a placeholder for an em dash in plain text editors.

---

4. To check en dashes, enter its punctuation (–) or enter ^= (caret code) or ^0150 (character code) in Find What. You can also select and en dash from the Special Characters

pull-down menu at the bottom of the Find and Replace dialog box to enter the ^= caret code.

REMINDER: Shortcut Keys for an en dash are CTRL + - NUMERIC KEYPAD (Windows) and OPT + HYPHEN (Mac). See Chapter 2, Shortcut Keys for Special Characters for more information.

---

5. Leave Replace With empty this time and just find the en dashes. Make sure the en dash is used correctly, and if it's not, change the punctuation directly in the manuscript.

6. If you feel it's needed, follow the same instructions to check the regular dashes or hyphens to make sure they are used properly.

Ellipsis

Manuscripts often contain ellipses typed as three separate periods (. . .), but the proper format is a single ellipsis character (...). Using three individual periods can cause formatting issues, especially in eBooks, where the periods may break across lines, so the reader could see two periods at the end of a line and one period at the beginning of the next line. Standardizing all ellipsis as one character or symbol prevents spacing errors.

In the following checklist, you'll use Find and Replace to convert all instances of three periods into the correct ellipsis character.

1. In the Find What field, enter three consecutive periods (. . .) with no space between them.

2. In Replace With, enter an actual ellipsis (…) or enter ^0133. Note, there is no ellipsis option under Special Characters.

REMINDER: Shortcut Keys for an ellipsis are ALT + CTRL + PERIOD (Windows) and OPT + SEMICOLON (Mac). See Chapter 2, Shortcut Keys for Special Characters for more information.

---

3. Click Replace All—MS Word will automatically replace three periods with an ellipsis. Or use Find Next and Replace to walk through the changes.

By now, you've covered the most common punctuation cleanup tasks that can clutter or destabilize a manuscript's formatting. This includes standardizing quotation marks (straight vs. curly), fixing inconsistent use of em and en dashes, and replacing three periods with proper ellipses. These offenders can lead to visual inconsistencies, poor readability, or formatting issues—especially during eBook conversion or professional typesetting.

Additional Hidden Characters to Watch For

Know that there are a few lesser-known elements that could still appear in your document. These include optional hyphens, non-breaking hyphens, and special symbols copied from web content or older file formats. If strange spacing or punctuation issues persist after completing this chapter, check the Symbol dialog box, as was discussed in Chapter 2 and the previous chapter.

By addressing the most visible and impactful punctuation issues now, you're laying the foundation for a polished, professional manuscript that will look clean on the page. This foundational work saves you time, frustration, and expense, preparing your manuscript for the next stage of editing or formatting. With these distractions gone, you're one step closer to a polished, publication-ready book. In the next chapter, you'll focus on standardizing display to further refine your manuscript.

Applying Styles for Consistency

Chapter 5

MANY WRITERS USE direct formatting—manually adjusting text properties like bold, italics, spacing, or indentation—which often leads to inconsistencies and makes global changes difficult. Instead, using styles in MS Word provides a structured way to apply consistent formatting throughout your document. A style is a predefined set of formatting rules, such as font, size, spacing, and indentation. By applying styles, you can format your manuscript uniformly with a single click. If changes are needed, updating the style will automatically apply those changes wherever the style is used, saving time and maintaining a clean, professional look.

Styles also improve document navigation by enabling MS Word's Navigation Pane, making it easy to move between chapters and sections. Additionally, they allow for an automatic table of contents generation, pulling headings directly from the document. By using styles, you create a well-structured manuscript that is easy to edit, format, and prepare for publication. In the next sections, you'll learn how to apply, modify, and create styles effectively.

This book introduces styles from a beginner's perspective, focusing on their practical use rather than an in-depth exploration of all their features. You won't need to master every aspect of styles—just enough to standardize text and create a few headers for easy navigation using the Navigation Pane. The goal is to ensure consistency in your manuscript while making it easier to edit, format, and structure for publishing. By learning a few essential style techniques, you'll streamline the cleanup process without getting lost in complex formatting options.

Applying Default Styles to Text

MS Word comes with a set of built-in styles that provide a simple way to format your manuscript consistently. These default styles, such as Normal, Heading 1, Heading 2, and so on, allow you to apply uniform formatting without manually adjusting font size, spacing, or alignment.

This section will guide you through the most efficient ways to apply styles throughout your manuscript, replace manual formatting with styles, and troubleshoot common style-related issues.

Since you already applied the Normal text style at the end of Chapter 2, you'll now add a heading style to a chapter or section title. This will show you how headers appear in the Navigation Pane and help you begin organizing your manuscript's structure.

1. Place the cursor within a line of text that represents a chapter title or main, top-level heading.

2. In the Styles Group on the Home Tab, click on the Heading 1 style. If you don't see the Heading 1 style, click on the

down arrow on the right (Windows) or below the listed styles (Mac). See the example image below.

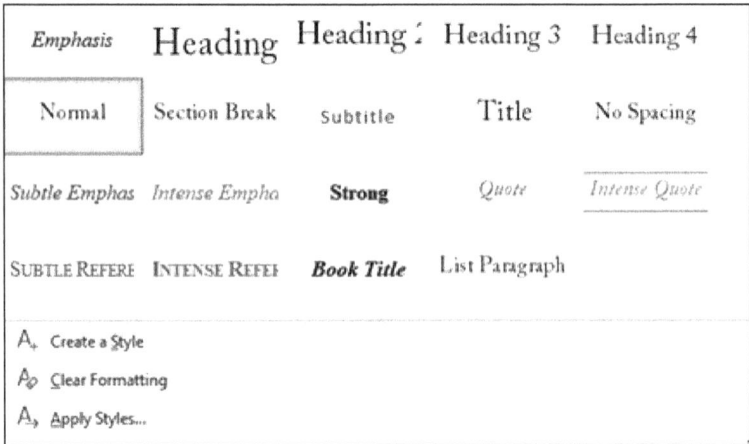

For faster formatting, use these Keyboard Shortcuts while the cursor is on the line where you want to apply a style:

- **Normal Style:** CTRL + SHIFT + N (Windows) / CMD + OPT + N (Mac) applies this style.

- **Heading Styles**: CTRL + ALT + 1, 2, or 3 (Windows) / CMD + OPT + 1, 2, or 3 (Mac) applies the Heading 1, Heading 2, or Heading 3 style respectively.

NOTE: Although we won't cover it, Keyboard Shortcuts are customizable. Their settings are found under the Format option when modifying a style. How to get there is covered in the next section.

As you learned in Chapter 2, the Normal style is used for the main body text of your manuscript, ensuring consistent font, size, and spacing throughout. Heading styles (such as Heading 1, Heading 2, and Heading 3) are designed for section titles and chapter headings. Applying heading styles not only formats your headers consistently, but it also places them in the Navigation Pane, making it easier to navigate through your document. You opened the Navigation Pane in Chapter 2, but here's a quick reminder how to do it.

- On both Windows and Mac, go to the View Tab on the Ribbon and check the Navigation Pane box in the Show Group.

- On Windows, if the Navigation Pane is closed, use the Keyboard Shortcut CTRL + F to open it directly.

3. Go to the Headings Tab and notice the title text in the list. Click on it and you'll jump to the page where the header displays.

Modifying Default Styles

One of the biggest advantages of using styles in MS Word is that when you modify a style, every instance of that style updates automatically throughout your document. This ensures consistent formatting without the need for tedious manual adjustments. Instead of individually changing fonts, spacing, or paragraph indents throughout your manuscript, you can modify the Normal style, and MS Word will apply the changes wherever that style is used.

Accessing the Style Modifier

Use this checklist to start adjusting the Normal style's font and paragraph formatting so you can see how the process works.

1. Go to the Home Tab and in the Styles Group, locate the Normal style.

2. Right-click on Normal, then choose Modify.

3. In the Modify Style dialog box, go to the bottom left and click on Format. The image below shows the Modify Style dialog box on Windows. It appears similar on Mac.

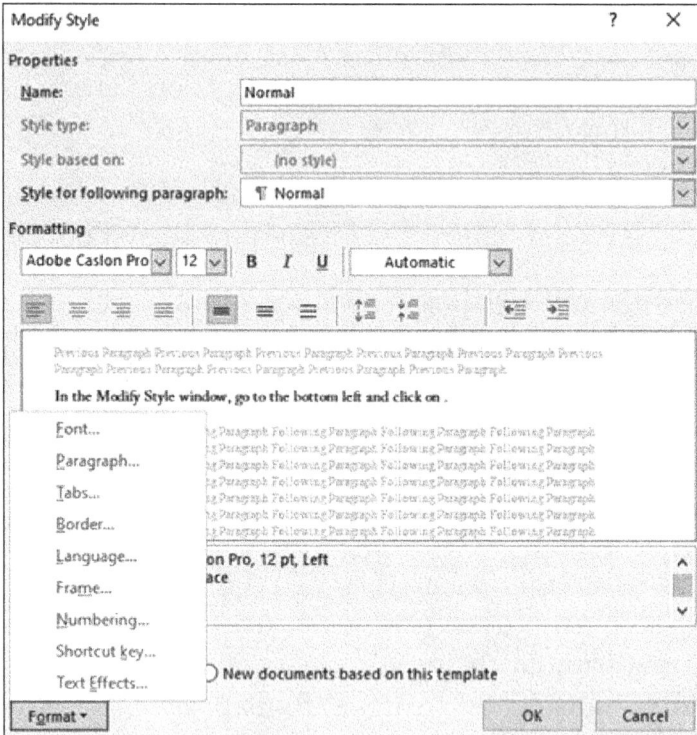

NOTE: The Format menu contains the same formatting options available in the Ribbon, so many of these settings should already be familiar. Also notice the Shortcut Key option, which was mentioned in the previous section.

Standard Font Styles and Their Uses

In professionally published books, especially in fiction and nonfiction print formats, serif fonts are the industry standard because they enhance readability in long blocks of text. Here are the most used fonts and their typical sizes as they appear in text so you can see what they look like:

- **Times New Roman Size 11 or 12 pt**: A classic serif font often used in manuscripts submitted to editors, agents, or publishers. It's widely accepted and highly readable.

- **Garamond Size 11 or 12 pt**: Elegant and traditional, Garamond is often used in printed novels and nonfiction. It takes up slightly less space than Times New Roman.

- **Minion Pro Size 11 pt**: Popular among professional typesetters for its readability and balanced look in print.

- **Adobe Caslon Pro Size 11 or 12 pt**: A favorite for book interiors, especially literary works, because of its timeless appearance and excellent legibility.

- **Georgia Size 11 or 12 pt**: Designed for screen reading but also looks good in print. Used in some self-published works due to its clarity.

- **Palatino Linotype / Book Antiqua Size 11 or 12 pt**: Often chosen for nonfiction and academic books. Slightly larger appearance makes it good for older readers.

IMPORTANT: Only fonts installed on your computer are available for selection in MS Word. Do a quick Google search or ask AI for instruction on installing fonts on Windows or Mac.

When formatting your manuscript, it's important to consider how the document will be used—whether you're submitting it to an agent or editor, preparing it for print, or formatting it for an eBook. Here is a quick guide to help you choose the right settings based on your manuscript's audience and destination:

- **Manuscript Submission**: Use Times New Roman, 12 pt, double-spaced. This is the industry standard for traditional manuscript submissions because it's easy to read, clean, and compatible with virtually every word processor and platform. However, you should always follow specific submission guidelines provided by agents and editors.

- **Print Book Interior Formatting**: Fonts like Adobe Caslon Pro or Garamond in 11–12 pt are commonly used in professionally typeset books. These serif fonts are highly readable and have a timeless, polished look. This print book uses 13 pt Adobe Caslon Pro, a little larger because it's easier to see and follow in a checklist format.

- **eBooks**: In most eBook formats, the font is controlled by the eReader device or app, not the one you embed. Choose a font like Adobe Caslon Pro and stay consistent with the font style. It's always better to let the reader have full control over font type and style because they know how they prefer to read.

Modifying the Normal Font Style

Now that you know all about standard fonts, here's how to change Normal style's font appearance. If you already know how to do this manually for selected text, you're already familiar with the process.

1. In the Modify Style dialog box, choose Font from the Format menu to open the Font settings shown in the image below on Windows. The dialog box looks similar on Mac.

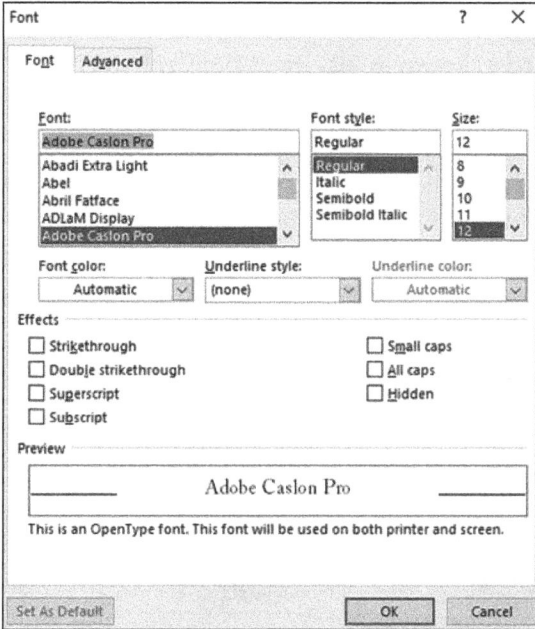

NOTE: The Font dialog box that opens is the same as the one accessed by clicking the Font Group's dialog box launcher on the Ribbon.

---

2. In the Font window, change the text size to 14 or something larger than the current setting, then adjust any other settings such as the font style to bold.

3. Click OK, then click OK again in the Modify Styles dialog box.

4. Notice how most of the text in the document, which is assigned the Normal style, updates instantly.

5. If you want to change the text back to the previous setting, hit CTRL + Z (Windows) or CMD + Z (Mac) to undo the style change. You can also use the Undo/Redo options in the Quick Access Toolbar.

6. If your manuscript doesn't use one of the standard fonts discussed in the previous section, you might want to repeat this checklist, changing the Normal style to a setting based on your needs.

Modifying the Paragraph Style

This checklist will guide you through updating the Normal Paragraph style for both fiction and nonfiction manuscripts. Since these formats have different layout conventions, understanding how to customize styles will help you adapt your document based on your publishing needs.

- **Fiction manuscripts** typically use indented paragraphs with no extra space between them. This format mirrors traditional print books and ensures smooth readability.

- **Nonfiction manuscripts** often use block paragraphs with extra spacing between them, making the text easier to scan, especially for instructional or academic writing.

Now here's how to change a paragraph's appearance for the Normal style for fiction and nonfiction.

1. Open the Modify Style dialog box as was done earlier.

2. Open the Format menu, then choose Paragraph. Again, the dialog box is similar on Windows and Mac.

3. Make sure you're on the Indents and Spacing Tab.

The Paragraph settings include alignment, indentions, spacing and more, as shown in the following image.

NOTE: The Paragraph dialog box that opens is the same as the one accessed by clicking the Paragraph Group's dialog box launcher on the Ribbon.

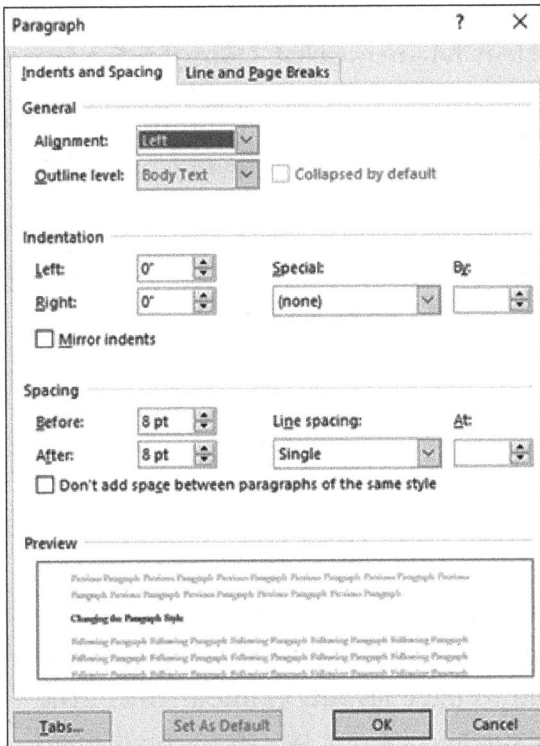

4. Adjust the settings according to the formatting style you need. The typical settings for fiction and nonfiction are found on the next page.

Fiction Manuscript (Double-Spaced)

For a standard fiction manuscript formatted for publication submission, use these normal paragraph settings:

- Alignment: Left
- Left and Right Indentions: 0"
- Special Indention: First Line by 0.5"
- Before and After Spacing: 0 pt
- Line Spacing: Double

Nonfiction Manuscript (Single-Spaced)

For a standard, single-spaced nonfiction manuscript, use these paragraph settings for the normal style:

- Alignment: Left
- Left and Right Indentions: 0"
- Special Indention: (none)
- Before and After Spacing: Both 8 pt
- Line Spacing: Single

While these are standard formatting guidelines, you can adjust them based on your personal preferences or publisher's requirements.

5. Optionally, click on the Line and Page Breaks Tab in the Paragraph dialog box to adjust how paragraphs behave in relation to page layout. While many of the settings here are self-explanatory, one worth highlighting is Page Break Before. Enabling this option ensures that any text using the style—such as a chapter heading—automatically starts on a new page. This is especially useful for long-form works and aligns with standard publishing practices for print books.

6. Click OK, then click OK on the Modify Style dialog box. The text adjusts to the new settings.

Modifying styles is a simple yet powerful way to ensure consistent formatting throughout your manuscript. With styles properly applied, your manuscript will be clean, professional, and easier to navigate—a crucial step in preparing it for editing, publishing, or submission. As you continue refining your document, you'll find that styles make formatting more efficient and eliminate the need for tedious manual changes.

Note on Shunn Manuscript Format

If you're preparing your manuscript for traditional submission, consider reviewing the Shunn Standard Manuscript Format. It's a widely accepted layout that includes double spacing, one-inch margins, standard font (like Courier or Times New Roman), specific header/footer details, and scene breaks marked by a centered hash (#). While Polished Pages helps you clean and standardize your document, Shunn format can offer guidance on final presentation when submitting to agents or editors. You can find the full guide at shunn.net/format.

Creating Styles

Now that you're familiar with applying and modifying styles, try creating a style with this checklist. The steps to start are a bit different on Windows and Mac, so follow the section for your computer type.

Windows: Start a New Style

Here you will create a new style.

1. Open the Style Group on the Home Tab to display the list of styles.

2. Choose Create a Style.

3. Name the style, then click on Modify and you'll open the Create New Style from Formatting dialog box.

Mac: Start a New Style

Here you will create a new style.

1. In the Style Group on the Ribbon, click on Styles Pane to open the settings in the right column.

2. Click on the New Style button to open the Create New Style from Formatting dialog box.

3. Enter a Name for the Style in the Name field.

4. Whether you are on Windows or Mac, the currently open dialog box used to create a new style behaves the same as the Modify Style dialog box. Make changes to the style like you did in earlier checklists.

While we won't go into all the other style settings and options, there are two additional settings worth mentioning:

Style Based On: This determines which existing style the new one inherits from. For example, if you base your style on Normal, it will use the same font and paragraph formatting unless you override specific options. Choosing the right base ensures consistency and saves time.

Style for Following Paragraph: This setting controls what style is automatically applied after you hit ENTER. For example, if you're creating a style for Chapter Titles, you might want the following paragraph to default back to Normal, so the body text format resumes automatically.

5. Once you've finished setting up the new style, click on OK.

6. When you're ready to apply the style, use the steps from *Applying Default Styles to Text* to locate it in the Styles Group and apply it to your selected text.

Creating your own styles gives you even greater control over how your manuscript looks and behaves. Once you've practiced with the basics—like naming a style, setting its formatting, and choosing the right base—it becomes much easier to build a consistent, professional document that's easy to update later. Whether you're styling chapter titles, subheadings, or special formatting blocks, using custom styles ensures your layout remains clean, organized, and easy to maintain through every phase of editing and production.

Manuscript Template

Before moving on to troubleshooting, it's helpful to understand how a standard draft manuscript is structured. Starting with a clean, professional layout makes editing and formatting much easier. The following examples show two common manuscript pages—the title page and the first page of content—along with guidance on how to format them using styles.

Title Page

In a typical draft manuscript, the title and author name appear on their own page, usually centered both horizontally and vertically as shown in the example below. This page should be simple and free of headers, footers, or page numbers. The book title is often written in all caps or title case, with the author's name placed several lines below.

Contact information (name, email, phone number) may also be included in the upper-left corner for agent or editor submissions, but it's often omitted in self-publishing drafts. This page should contain no extra formatting like bold or italics. In layout and cleanup, this page is one of the easiest to style consistently, and the sample on the previous page even includes manual formatting.

Author's Name   000,000 Words
Address
City, State, Zip Code
Phone Number
Email Address

                         TITLE

                     Series Title #1

                          By

                        Author

Author information appears at the top left of the title page and is formatted using single-spaced text with no additional space above or below each line. The font is Times New Roman, 12 pt—matching the standard manuscript body text

Word count appears at the top right and is manually formatted. Tabs are inserted after the author's name to align the word count on the right side of the page. As mentioned earlier in the book, manual formatting is sometimes the simplest solution, especially for one-time layout elements like this.

Title information appears in two different styles: one for the centered title and one for the series title and author name. Although all text is set to double spacing, the style for the book title includes 100 points of space before it, allowing it to sit lower on the page for balanced, professional placement.

Reminder, to create a title page with no header or footer—separate from the rest of your manuscript—you'll need to set the section to have a different first page. You did this in reverse, removing this separation in Chapter 2.

1. In MS Word, go to the Layout tab (Windows) or Document Elements > Layout (Mac).

2. Open the Page Setup dialog box. Under the Layout tab, check the box for Different First Page.

This allows you to remove headers and footers from the title page without affecting the rest of the document. It's an essential step if your manuscript includes a title page and you want the actual content to start cleanly on the following page.

Chapter Start Page

The first page of the manuscript usually begins with the chapter number or title, which should be centered horizontally and formatted with a heading style (such as Heading 1) for easy navigation. The text begins a few lines below, with body text set to the Normal style. For most drafts, especially those submitted for agents or editors, this first page also includes a header containing the author's last name, the manuscript title (shortened if long), and a page number—right-aligned.

This header usually appears on all manuscript pages except the title page. Page numbering typically starts at page 1 on the first page of the actual manuscript content, not the title page or dedication.

Author's Last Name / Book Title / 1

Chapter 1

Lorem ipsum dolor sit amet, consectetur adipiscing elit. Integer nec odio. Praesent libero. Sed cursus ante dapibus diam. Sed nisi. Nulla quis sem at nibh elementum imperdiet. Duis sagittis ipsum. Praesent mauris. Fusce nec tellus sed augue semper porta. Mauris massa. Vestibulum lacinia arcu eget nulla.

Lorem ipsum dolor sit amet, consectetur adipiscing elit. Integer nec odio. Praesent libero. Sed cursus ante dapibus diam. Sed nisi. Nulla quis sem at nibh elementum imperdiet. Duis sagittis ipsum. Praesent mauris. Fusce nec tellus sed augue semper porta. Mauris massa. Vestibulum lacinia arcu eget nulla.

There's no single way to format a manuscript, but the example shown here reflects a clean, professional layout widely accepted by agents, editors, and book formatters. Whether submitting traditionally or self-publishing, starting with a consistent format helps simplify editing and production.

Now that you've mastered how to apply, modify, and create styles, let's look at some of the issues you might encounter and how to fix them.

Troubleshooting Style Issues

Even when applying styles correctly, you may encounter unexpected formatting issues that disrupt the consistency of your manuscript. These problems often occur when manual formatting conflicts with style settings, or when text imported from another document carries over hidden formatting. Here are common style-related problems and how to fix them.

Style Not Applying Correctly

Follow these steps if you apply a style, but the text doesn't change, or only some aspects of the formatting update.

1. Select the affected text.

2. Go to the Home Tab, and in the Font Group, click on the Clear All Formatting option to remove any residual manual formatting.

You can also use these Keyboard Shortcuts:

- **Windows**: Press CTRL + SPACEBAR

- **Mac**: Press CMD + SPACEBAR

3. Reapply the desired style from the Styles Group on the Home Tab.

NOTE: Clearing formatting removes any direct modifications that may be overriding the applied style. After doing this, your text will fully adopt the settings defined by the style.

Styles Missing from the Styles Group

Sometimes the Styles Group displays only a limited number of options, such as just Heading 1, Heading 2, and Heading 3, while hiding the other headings. This is done to keep the Styles Group neat and easy to navigate, making commonly used styles quicker to find without overwhelming the list.

If some styles are missing from the Styles Group, follow these steps to restore any missing styles:

1. Go to the Home Tab.

2. Follow the next steps based on your computer type:

Windows: Add Style to Group

Here you will add missing styles to the Styles Group.

1. Click the additional options arrow in the Styles Group to open the Styles Pane.

2. Page through the styles and find the missing style.

If the style is missing from the Styles Pane list, select Options. At the top of the dialog box, choose All Styles. Also check "Show next heading when previous level is used," which is helpful for manuscripts with many header levels.

3. Choose Add to Styles Gallery.

Mac: Add Style to Group

Here you will add missing styles to the Styles Group.

1. In the Styles Group, click on the Styles Pane option.

2. Choose All Styles from the List menu.

3. Hover near the far right of the needed style to expose the menu arrow. Click on it, then choose Modify Style.

4. Go the the bottom left and check Add to Quick Style List, then click OK.

5. On either Windows or Mac, go to the Styles Group and the style will be in the list.

By ensuring that all necessary styles are available, you gain greater flexibility in formatting your manuscript. Having access to a full range of styles allows you to apply consistent formatting more efficiently, making your document easier to edit, navigate, and prepare for final publication.

A Professional Polished Manuscript

Conclusion

CLEANING UP A manuscript is an essential step in preparing your work for editing, submission, or publication. Throughout this book, you've learned how to remove unnecessary formatting, standardize punctuation, and apply styles to create a well-structured and professional document. These techniques not only ensure your manuscript is consistent and easy to read but also make the formatting process smoother for editors, book designers, and publishing platforms.

Taking the time to clean and format your manuscript correctly prevents many common issues that can arise when converting your document for different formats, such as eBooks or print. Whether you're submitting your manuscript to an agent, editor, or self-publishing platform, a well-organized document helps establish credibility and professionalism, making your work stand out.

While MS Word's tools provide powerful ways to format and refine your manuscript, remember that no automated process replaces a final human review. As a final step, read through your document carefully, checking for lingering errors or inconsistencies. If needed, revisit key sections of this book to fine-tune your formatting before moving forward.

Now that you have a polished manuscript, you're ready for the next step in your publishing journey. Whether that's sending your book to an editor, formatting it for print, or preparing an eBook, your clean and structured document will make the process smoother, faster, and more professional. Keep these formatting techniques in mind for future projects, and you'll save time and frustration every time you prepare a manuscript.

Your book is ready—now go share your story with the world!

Glossary

Anchor (Object Anchor): A symbol in MS Word indicating that a floating object (e.g., image or text box) is tied to a specific paragraph.

AutoCorrect: A feature in MS Word that automatically corrects spelling, capitalization, punctuation, and formatting errors as you type.

Caret Code (Control Code): A special character in MS Word's Find and Replace feature that represents non-printing elements or formatting, such as paragraph marks (^p) or tabs (^t).

Character Code: A numerical value assigned to a symbol, punctuation mark, or character (often ASCII or Unicode) that can be used in Find and Replace when formatted as a caret code (e.g., ^0133 for an ellipsis).

Dialog Box Launcher: A small arrow in the bottom-right corner of some Ribbon Groups (Windows only) that opens a full settings dialog for that Group (e.g., Font or Paragraph settings).

Direct Formatting: Manually applying formatting (such as bold, italic, or font changes) to individual pieces of text instead of using a style.

Ellipsis Character (…): A single punctuation character used to indicate a pause, trailing thought, or omission. Unlike typing three separate periods (...), the ellipsis character is treated as one unit, which prevents it from breaking across lines in digital formats like eBooks. It is inserted using the shortcut Alt + Ctrl + . (Windows) or Option + ; (Mac), or with the character code ^0133 in Find and Replace.

Em Dash vs. En Dash: The em dash (—) is a long dash used to indicate a break in thought or to add emphasis—similar to parentheses or a dramatic pause. The en dash (–) is shorter and used primarily to show ranges (e.g., 1990–2000) or connections (e.g., Denver–Chicago flight). Em dashes are commonly used in fiction and narrative writing. In Word, the em dash is inserted using Ctrl + Alt + - (Windows) or Shift + Option + Hyphen (Mac); the en dash uses Ctrl + - (Windows) or Option + Hyphen (Mac).

Field Code: A placeholder for dynamic data like page numbers or dates. You can toggle visibility with ALT + F9 (Windows).

Find and Replace: A tool in MS Word used to locate specific words, symbols, or formatting and replace them automatically throughout the document.

Formatting Marks (Non-printing Characters): Symbols like paragraph marks, spaces, tabs, and page breaks that appear in your document when formatting marks are turned on. These marks help you see hidden formatting issues.

Header/Footer: Sections at the top (header) and bottom (footer) of each page where you can insert elements like page numbers, titles, or author names

Hyphenation: The process of breaking words at the end of a line using a hyphen. Can be manual, optional, or automatic.

Keep Lines Together: A paragraph formatting option that prevents a paragraph from breaking across pages.

Keep with Next: A setting that keeps a paragraph on the same page as the next one—often used for headings.

Line Break (Manual Line Break): A soft return inserted by pressing SHIFT + ENTER. Moves text to a new line without starting a new paragraph.

Manuscript: The complete, written version of a book or document before it has been professionally edited, formatted, or published. A manuscript typically includes all chapters, scenes, and relevant content in a draft or near-final state, and may be submitted to agents, editors, or book formatters for review or production.

Navigation Pane: A panel on the side of your document window that shows headings, pages, or search results—useful for navigating long documents.

Nonbreaking Hyphen: A hyphen that keeps the words on either side together on the same line. Inserted with CTRL + SHIFT + - (Windows).

Normal Style: The default paragraph style in MS Word that controls the base font, spacing, and layout of body text.

Object: Any inserted item in MS Word that is not plain text, like a shape, table, chart, or image.

Optional Hyphen: A hyphen that only appears if the word breaks at the end of a line. Inserted with CTRL + - (Windows).

Page Break: A formatting element that forces the start of a new page. Manual page breaks are inserted with CTRL + ENTER.

Paragraph Mark: A formatting mark that appears at the end of each paragraph (¶). It indicates where you've pressed Enter to start a new paragraph.

Ribbon: The toolbar at the top of the MS Word window, organized into tabs (Home, Insert, Layout, etc.) and groups of related commands.

Section Break: A break that divides a document into separate sections, each of which can have its own formatting (e.g., margins, headers/footers, page orientation).

Shortcut Keys: A combination of keyboard keys used to quickly perform a command or action in a software program without using menus or a mouse. In Microsoft Word, shortcut keys speed up tasks like saving a file, applying formatting, or opening Find and Replace. For example, Ctrl + S (Windows) or Command + S (Mac) saves your document instantly. Shortcut keys improve efficiency and are especially helpful during cleanup and editing.

Smart Quotes: Also called curly quotes, these are quotation marks that curl toward the enclosed text (" " for double quotes, ' ' for single). Smart Quotes replace the straight, typewriter-style quotation marks (" or ') and are considered the standard in professional publishing. In Word, Smart Quotes are enabled through AutoCorrect settings and ensure proper punctuation throughout your manuscript.

Soft Return: See "Manual Line Break."

Style: A predefined set of formatting options (like font, size, spacing) applied to text. Styles provide consistency and simplify global formatting changes.

Style Based On: A setting in a custom style that determines which other style it inherits its formatting from.

Style for Following Paragraph: A setting that defines which style MS Word should apply after you press Enter while using a particular style.

Tab Character: A formatting mark represented by an arrow that indicates where the Tab key was used to indent or align text.

Track Changes: A feature that shows edits, insertions, and deletions made to a document—useful for collaboration and reviewing revisions.

White Space (in Find and Replace): A caret code (^w) that represents any amount of space between words or punctuation—useful when cleaning up extra spacing.

References

OpenAI. ChatGPT. March 14 version. Accessed March–April 2025. https://chat.openai.com.

Palmquist, Mike, and Barbara Wallraff. *In Conversation: A Writer's Guidebook*. Bedford/St. Martin's, 2014.

Microsoft Word and related terms/screenshots are trademarks of Microsoft Corporation.

"Microsoft Word Help & Learning." *Microsoft Support.* https://support.microsoft.com

Selected tips and methods originally appeared in training material created by the author for ArmLin House Productions.

Acknowledgements

Writing this book was a long but rewarding journey, and I couldn't have done it without the support, patience, and encouragement of the people around me.

To the writers, editors, and clients I've worked with over the years—you inspired this book with your questions, challenges, and dedication to telling your stories. Every formatting disaster and late-night manuscript rescue helped shape this guide into something truly useful.

A heartfelt thank-you to my creative and personal cheerleaders who kept me focused, caffeinated, and laughing through every round of edits.

And finally, a big shoutout to ChatGPT, my ever-patient brain-storming and editing partner. You never blinked at a single formatting mark or style question (and trust me, there were plenty).

About the Author

Wendy Spurlin is a seasoned author, editor, and artist with more than 40 years of experience helping writers refine their craft. She has edited countless manuscripts, led critique groups, and taught writers how to strengthen their work through writing and feedback. With 8 years of service in the U.S. Air Force, 30 years in technology, and over 20 years in business marketing, Wendy brings a rare blend of discipline, tech know-how, and creative insight to everything she does.

As the founder of ArmLin House Productions and creator of Business Author Boot Camp, Wendy helps authors and entrepreneurs transform ideas into professionally published books and media. She is especially known for creating instructional manuals that simplify complex processes—like this one—through her clear, engaging teaching style.

Wendy also writes fiction under the pen name Winnie Jean Howard, best known for the Angels Dark and Dumb series, which blends horror and humor in a voice that's both unsettling and sharply witty. Her fiction explores the darker side of human nature with a comedic twist, earning praise for its originality and memorable characters.

A lifelong artist, Wendy illustrates children's books, creates haunting horror art, and produces abstract pieces that explore emotion and imagination. She is also an experienced video editor for social media content, blending visual storytelling with marketing strategy. Whether she's illustrating a whimsical picture book or formatting a manuscript for print, Wendy's work combines artistic vision with technical skill.

When she's not working, you'll find her hiking, enjoying a good glass of wine, watching horror movies and documentaries, or discovering new culinary spots. Through her books, art, and coaching, Wendy continues to inspire, educate, and empower creators at every stage of their journey.

More Info

armlinhouse.com

@armlinhouse on
Instagram
Facebook
X
@armlinhouseproductions
Substack

@wendyspurlin on
Bluesky
Amazon
GoodReads

www.ingramcontent.com/pod-product-compliance
Lightning Source LLC
Chambersburg PA
CBHW060250030426
42335CB00014B/1647